W9-BLL-058

WITHDRAWN

Venice
for
Lovers

*for Nicholas, Julia,
Isabella, Henri and Jacob*

Venice
for
Lovers

Louis Begley
Anka Muhlstein

GROVE PRESS
NEW YORK

Originally published in German by marebuchverlag,
in Hamburg, Germany in 2003 as *Les Clefs de Venise*

First published in English in Great Britain
in 2005 by Haus Publishing Limited, London

Printed in the United States of America
Published simultaneously in Canada

ISBN-10: 0-8021-1875-5
ISBN-13: 978-0-8021-1875-2

Grove Press
an imprint of Grove/Atlantic, Inc.
841 Broadway
New York, NY 10003
Distributed by Publishers Group West
www.groveatlantic.com

08 09 10 11 12   10 9 8 7 6 5 4 3 2 1

Contents

Preface

Beginning in 2001 or early 2002, we were asked repeatedly by the publisher of the German version of this volume, who knew our deep attachment to Venice, and liked our work, whether we would jointly write for a book about it for him. We answered always that we are not travel or guidebook writers, and that, in any event, we do not write together. Anka is a historian and biographer; Louis is a novelist. She writes in French, and he writes in English. We did not think that such a thing could be done. In addition, we pleaded commitment to other projects, a solid reason, especially since Louis was then still practicing law full time. The publisher persisted. In the spring of 2002, the text of a speech Louis gave at a benefit event for Save Venice, a charity devoted to the protection of Venetian monuments, came into our publisher's hands.

We have the kernel, he told us, the kernel of your book. That kernel was, in somewhat different form, the essay about the use novelists have made of Venice, which is the third part of this volume. All we need now, our publisher continued, is a very personal piece by Anka about her Venice, and a short story with a Venetian theme by Louis.

And so the book took shape.

It was by then summer. Anka had finished the research for her *Elisabeth I et Marie Stuart ou les périls du marriage,* which appeared in October 2004, and was only beginning to write. Louis had almost completed his most recent novel, *Shipwreck*. The charm and wiles of our publisher prevailed. We agreed to this most unusual project, a work by a

French and an English- speaking writer that would initially appear in German.

We have reconsidered and revised our pieces for this English edition. A writer's work is never done; we could have gone on revising forever. One always feels that one should. But then no work would come to be published. We stand by what we wrote two years ago. The experience of Venice is an intensely personal one, if only because *la serenissima* is so mysterious and wins one over so completely. That is what we have tried to convey in our very different ways. We have also hoped to infect our readers with our own love for Venice, which runs very deep, and has brought us great happiness.

Anka Muhlstein
Louis Begley

The Keys to Venice

by Anka Muhlstein
translated by Anne Wyburd

For the last 20 years we have spent a fortnight's holiday in Venice each year – either in the autumn or the spring – holidays which over the years have acquired Colette's meaning: 'a holiday is working elsewhere', because during these periods in Venice my husband has been able to write without incessant interruptions. He has the enormous advantage of being a novelist and having everything in his head. I, poor biographer, need books, dictionaries and encyclopedias for my work. Since we hate travelling with a portable library, I do not always write there, but I read, correct and rewrite. This has not always been the case. Before Louis started writing in 1989, we spent long periods walking, losing our way, looking at pictures, going to concerts or negotiating to get into places closed to tourists like us. Among our triumphs we count a visit to the Biblioteca Marciana to see the first editions of Dante – won after claiming a completely imaginary friendship with the director of the New York Public Library – and an hour spent in the Baptistery of Saint Mark's, accompanied by a functionary of the basilica who was moved by our supplications, and gracious enough to respond to our thanks by saying that our pleasure in contemplating 'his' treasures consoled him for the spectacle of the troop of tourists - *la gregge di pecore* (the flock of sheep) – who invaded his church, shuffling their feet and damaging the wonderful pavement. But we did not always succeed. During the years when the doors of San Sebastiano only opened for a brief mass and no exceptions permitted, the guardian of San Sebastiano was impervious to our charms, our pleas as visitors

from afar and our passion for Veronese. The porter
of the Patriarchal Seminary and the guardian of
the Conservatory were equally intransigent.

Step by step we got to know the city, until I no
longer needed to walk about with a map in my
hand. First of all I knew that, contrary to what I
had thought to begin with, it is impossible to get
lost in Venice – one only has to follow the flow to
find oneself back under the clock tower in Saint
Mark's Square or at the foot of the Rialto Bridge –
and then I had my landmarks: a shop window, a
sign, a stone lion guarding a balcony, a sculpted
door reminded me where to turn. In fact the game
now consisted in following non-tourist itineraries
and avoiding Saint Mark's and its surroundings
before 6 pm. If one wanted to go into the Basilica
one had either to attend Vespers or to slip in by a
side entrance, put on a solemn face and explain to
the doorkeeper that one had come to say one's
prayers. The walk towards Santa Madonna dell'Orto

involved discovering a silent Venice populated by housewives, children and old people in slippers, and a stroll along the Canareggio meant experiencing a more active, working-class Venice. San Francesco della Vigna or the far side of the Arsenal also offered *campi* where passers-by walked with the quick, decisive step of local residents, expert at avoiding the flights of ubiquitous footballs. Venice had become familiar to us; our first slightly frenetic curiosity had been satisfied. Working in the afternoons (we always devoted our mornings to walking) was the sign that we were now at home in Venice. We had changed, but one of our principles had remained unaltered: we did not want to meet anybody.

Trailing through the alleys of the city in a group while checking that everyone else was following, making appointments which were doomed to be missed, because someone would make a mistake over the vaporetto ('the 7 has become the 82 and the landing-stage has been moved', they would explain pathetically), while others would confuse the Gesuati with the Gesuiti, the Palazzo Bembo with the Bembo-Boldù or even the Palazzo Contarini with the Contarini-Fasan, the Contarini-Michiel or any of the six other Contarini palaces, spending the evening gossiping or talking politics with friends we see all the time in New York or Paris while one is absorbed in one's real or fictitious characters – no, we did not want that. Of course, it is foolish to think one can avoid people completely in this very small town. We were lucky to have an alibi in the charming person of one of our nieces who had settled in Venice. Any attempt to suggest a meeting was countered with 'I am so sorry, we are dining – or lunching, or taking tea – with Marie'. So we continued to see nobody except those we saw every day and even twice a day - that is, the proprietors and head waiters of the restaurants we frequented.

At the risk of seeming to be a little set in our ways, I have to admit to another of our rules: when we find a restaurant we like, we take it unreservedly to our hearts. We love going to the same place every evening; the menu holds no surprises for us (anyhow, Louis is never happier than when eating the same food every day), we are given a friendly welcome and feel at home, with the unparalleled advantage of not having to do the washing up. But in Venice, as everywhere in Italy, one has to take into account the *riposo settimanale* (weekly closing), which shuts down every establishment for two days a week. So a certain rotation is necessary for survival. In the course of our 20 Venetian years we have adopted four eating-places and the daily routine of the different restaurateurs, chefs or head waiters has been an unsurpassable means of getting to know the city and its inhabitants.

The first to seduce us was Signor Ernesto. Venice is a city which goes to bed early. When evening comes, the countless tourists milling around Saint Mark's Square leave for the *terra firma*.

The tour companies' plans for the day involve an early start – their clients are not there to enjoy themselves; once they have signed up for culture they should be ready for instruction from an early hour. Not surprisingly, therefore, their evenings are cut short. One day we planned to go to the opera and, as we like dining after the performance, we decided to walk around the Fenice quarter in search of a place which might stay open late. We noticed in one of the tiny streets nearby (called, rather disturbingly, the Calle dei Assassini) a place so unobtrusive that one could easily have missed it – a long, narrow room furnished in pale wood, its walls hung with framed banknotes. Through the window we saw a rather corpulent man helped by a very thin younger one laying the tables. We tapped lightly on the door. He raised his eyes and came to open it. 'Is it possible to have a late dinner here?' asked Louis. 'We are going to the opera this evening.' 'You are in luck', he replied. 'La June is singing this evening. They are doing *Beatrice Cenci* tonight, aren't they? Of course I shall expect you. Don't worry. But tell me, do you like wine, red wine?' Our knowledge of Italian was equal to understanding a question as simple as that and we responded with enthusiasm. 'Excellent, I shall have *un vino di riserva, capo di stato* ready for you.'

I still remember with enchantment the voice and the beauty of June Anderson, whom we had not heard before. I do not remember the intricacies of the plot very clearly, except for the rage of the assassin (or was it the executioner?) in his red gloves, but I do remember very precisely our arrival at Ernesto's. We were the only guests. On a table stood a full carafe – one of those bell-mouthed Italian carafes, flanked by a black bottle. 'Italian wine, heady wine, you understand, needs to breathe before it can be appreciated.' Ernesto had trusted us and had uncorked and decanted a superb bottle of Amarone. 'Now, did she sing well?

Oh, I am so sad not to have heard her.' And he offered us a menu. A surprising menu for Venice: not a hint of fish, no crab, no prawn, no cuttle-fish, but a serious choice of meat. A thick, breaded pork cutlet cooked with vinegar, *steak au poivre* or *alla campagnola* and, quite unexpectedly, a hamburger of hand-chopped fillet, which he recommended before disappearing into what I would hesitate to call a kitchen – an area filled by a huge stove with six burners and lined with shelves, so tiny that it looked absolutely impossible for two people to move around in it, let alone prepare a meal for 30. To tell the truth, the restaurant was hardly larger than half a railway dining-car but it had another, mysterious dimension: the seats were so designed that they could be moved like pieces of a jigsaw puzzle to create tables for either four or eight. Ernesto and the young man rearranged them so rapidly that they might have been performing a conjuring trick.

My husband declared that he had never eaten such a good hamburger and we gave full marks to the pasta with gorgonzola which preceded it. We offered Ernesto a glass of his own wine and decided to come back the following day at a more civilised hour. That time the restaurant was full of a fashionable crowd, chatting merrily in Italian, French or English. Clearly the groups of diners knew each other and Ernesto's prices spared him the presence of thrifty tourists, happy with a plate of pasta and a glass of beer. At lunchtime the atmosphere was very different. From noon on the room was full of sober-suited Venetian gentlemen - antiquarians, doctors or lawyers from the neighbourhood, who had their own customs and probably even their own napkin rings. Ernesto, who called them all by name, suggested a *plat du jour*, which consisted in a savoury remake of yesterday's leftovers. For a few hours the restaurant was like a family pension.

In the evenings we were often the last customers, and once dessert and coffee were served we would invite Ernesto to finish the bottle with us. His limited French was on a level with our approximate Italian and we managed to understand each other. He had started earning his living as a waiter at the end of the 1950s, at a time when Venice was dormant in the winter. He therefore had to work through two different seasons: in the summer he was to be found first at the Saturnia and then the Caravelle in Venice and in the winter in Germany or at the Sunbeach at Aix-les-Bains. 'A hard life', I said to him, and he shrugged his shoulders and laughed. 'Not so bad.' He came from a family of fishermen in San Pietro in Volta, a village on the narrow, three kilometre-long island of Pellestrina to the south of the Lido, and had decided he did not want to grow old chasing after fish from a boat. He preferred running among tables and saving up steadily. In fact, he had been able to marry in

1964 at the age of 23. His wife and two daughters and he lived with his father and his aunt in the family house, which he had repainted in brick red. He had tiled the floors and put in a bathroom – a modern bathroom with a bidet, which caused a scandal among the neighbours. 'What is the bidet for?' asked his visitors. 'That Ernesto, he must have learned some dirty tricks in France.'

On 4 November 1966 the rhythm of his existence fell apart when Venice and its surroundings were engulfed by the most terrible flood of the century. Ernesto never talked about the details of that catastrophe; he preferred conversations about œnology or opera and most particularly about his beloved Verdi, but in 1996 he gave us a slim volume in which a Venetian journalist, Roberto Bianchin, traced the course of the disaster by following the daily life of his friend Ernesto. Having read it, I was stupefied. During days of *aqua alta* (high water) I had walked over the gangways made of wooden planks fastened to 50 cm-high trestles, which are put up quickly when the water overflows into the low-lying quarters of the city, but I had never imagined what a flood would mean to a city built on water. I went on questioning Ernesto until I could put together the story of his life during those dramatic days.

On Thursday 3 November, the day before he was due to leave for France, he and his wife Liliana had taken the morning boat from San Pietro to Chioggia, a port situated at the southern end of the lagoon and linked to the *terra firma* by a bridge. Thursday was market-day in Chioggia and Ernesto needed a new pair of shoes, comfortable shoes with crêpe soles to keep his feet warm and dry. They came home in the afternoon with the new shoes wrapped in the pink pages of a sporting newspaper. It was raining, the tide was rising, the wind was blowing very strongly and the grey daylight was fading. Ernesto and his family went to bed early. At midnight he was awakened by a group of fishermen arguing under his window. He pulled on his jeans and sweater and went down barefoot to see what was going on. When he stepped onto the pavement outside his house he saw the water already lapping against the walls. That could happen at very high tides but in such case the water never failed to go down in a few hours. In fact, Ernesto and the fishermen were worried. The water level should already have started to sink but, on the contrary, it was still rising, slowly and silently. Squalls of rain shook the house. Ernesto went back to bed; there was nothing else to do. But at dawn he leapt up. Was that loud bang an explosion? A clap of thunder? Worse, the dyke had given way. The long stone cordon which protected the island and the city from the sea had been ripped apart by the water and had collapsed. Looking out from the windows all one could see was the sea. Ernesto went to work at once. The ground floor was flooded. He rolled up his trousers and started taking everything he could carry on his back to safety on the top floor. He went up and down the stairs as quickly as he could but his efforts were in vain. The water rose and rose. The family took refuge in the attic, where fishing nets were fastened to the walls — those nets which women spend hours mending. They would have to leave the house, but how?

Suddenly they heard shouts. Two farm workers swaying about in a flat-bottomed boat called a *saltafossi*, had come to fetch them. The order to evacuate had been given. A ship was anchored further out to take residents to the Lido but only the smallest craft could come in close to the houses. Come quickly, only one bag each. Ernesto took a blanket, a bottle of milk for the children and some stale bread. His wife seized her earrings and rings and the small amount of money there was in the house. There was no point in weighing oneself down. The hardest thing was to convince his father to leave his home. On the ship Ernesto found his sister with her five children, his mother, friends and neighbours. Four thousand people were rescued in a few hours. Only a few obstinate youngsters, intoxicated with adventure and with the wine they were swigging from the bottles, refused to leave and stayed clinging to the roofs.

Landing at the Lido was difficult. All the pontoons had been torn away by a raging sea. It took several attempts to disembark the rescued passengers. Buses were waiting for them and through deep puddles and small pools they reached the shelter of the hospital – not a very comforting shelter. Like Venice and the neighbouring islands, the Lido was plunged in darkness – no electricity, no heating, no food and one bed per family in the large reception hall. His baby daughters were crying. Ernesto had thought of bringing milk for them but not their bottles. How were they going to feed the babies? A nurse, busy giving out blankets, was no help at all. Babies' bottles were in another building but it was inaccessible. Ernesto rummaged in the pocket of his soaking wet trousers and pulled out the damp, carefully folded ten thousand lire note, the note reserved for his journey to Aix-les-Bains that very day. He passed it to the woman. Half an hour later she brought him a candle and two bottles. The little girls went to sleep next to their mother on the bed. Ernesto stretched out on the floor.

On Saturday morning he got up in the grey dawn and joined a group of men standing in the doorway of the room, gloomy but relieved. 'It's over, the water is going down, the wind has turned.' 'And the island?' 'It's still there.' And Venice?

Completely isolated from the rest of Italy, Venice had passed through an appalling night. For twelve hours on end the water had remained at two metres above sea level. No help arrived from outside. The authorities, taken completely by surprise – nothing in the weather forecasts had indicated the force of the wind or the tide – had only been able to evacuate a few hundred old people at risk in their ground-floor rooms. A city like Venice, where transport goes by water, is much more vulnerable to flood than others. When the Seine overflowed in Paris in 1911 and some districts were under more than a metre of water, the inhabitants went around in boats. That is impossible in Venice. Boats cannot take to the streets, because they are blocked by bridges, nor to the canals, because when the water level goes up spectacularly there is not enough space for them to pass under the bridges. The city is therefore completely paralysed, and the sick and handicapped have to be carried to safety on men's backs. No food at all can be brought in, because it cannot be unloaded, and the dangers of an epidemic are increased by the fact that flooded markets burst open to disgorge floating carcasses of animals, poultry and fish, and rotting fruit and vegetables. Some irresponsible Venetians served the fish they collected from the canals and some criminal vendors sold drowned chickens they found floating in front of their doors. The sanitary authorities immediately embarked on a general disinfection programme and a campaign of preventative vaccination.

Doctors, nurses and Red Cross representatives began arriving at the Lido. The victims were to be transferred to another building. Ernesto then decided to find his father and return with him to San Pietro, to see whether their house was still standing. They left the women and children at the Lido. At the landing-stage they found a boat prepared to take them to the village. When they disembarked, they saw their roof in the distance – a great relief. They walked slowly along the ravaged street, cluttered with a jumble of furniture, cookers and old television sets. The guts of every house had been torn out and lay on the broken pavement. It would have been nice to say that they had arrived at their front door, but the house no longer had a door;

only the walls and chimney remained – and a metre of mud. The two men rolled up their sleeves and trouser legs and set to work without wasting a moment complaining. They had no shovel, no tool of any kind; they scooped up the mud in their hands and filled a rusty old bin, which they emptied into the lagoon. Ernesto stopped for a moment to walk around in search of news. He came across the two farm workers who had rescued them the night before and had not left the island after helping to evacuate the residents. They were walking around with fishing-nets, those little nets that children play with on the beach. Bass, swept in by the tide, could be found by the dozen on the quay, a little stunned but still alive. They were easy to catch. 'Want one, Ernesto?'

Ernesto dug out a wooden case which he broke up for kindling. He gutted and scaled his fish and speared it on the ferrule of an old umbrella. When evening came the two dirty and exhausted men squatted by the fire which burnt their faces, and ate their bass in their fingers. 'Amazing, that bass', said Ernesto to his journalist friend 30 years later, 'Amazing. The best I have ever eaten. I have never tasted a better one.' I never asked him, but I have always wondered whether his decision not to serve fish in his restaurant originated from the impossibility of finding one as good.

Of course Ernesto had to postpone his departure for France that year. He had to rebuild everything with his own hands: doors, windows and furniture, and repaint the house. The walls had to be reinforced and the floors washed and washed again with large buckets of water. He was starting from scratch. He had to borrow money for the bare essentials, because the aid given to the flood victims only amounted to 200,000 lire. But he lacked neither courage nor energy. In 1967 a third daughter was born and the family moved to Santa Maria del Giglio in Venice, where they are still living. He stopped going abroad for the winter season after 1968, because tourists had begun coming to Venice all through the year and there was no lack of work. In partnership with two friends he opened a large restaurant, Ala, opposite the church of Santa Maria del Giglio, whose façade is decorated with bas reliefs plans of Zara, Candia, Padua, Rome, Corfu and Spálato. Five years later he launched out on his own and bought a *vini* (wine bar) called Da Arturo, where he meant to stay for two years, but 2003 marks his thirtieth anniversary there. The name has remained unchanged.

Now that he had left San Pietro, from a distance it seemed to him charming and he incessantly urged us to spend a day there. 'You will see how pretty it is, with the houses painted in every colour – red, ochre and green – the square church, the vines and the vegetable gardens.' We listened but we have not been there yet. The biggest surprise came on an October Monday, the day we arrived in

Venice. 'You left New York on the day of the marathon', he told us. My daughter is a great sportswoman. She trains regularly and dreams of running in New York.' This was Raffaella, the middle daughter. The youngest, Elisabetta, was an architect and the only one of the three sisters living in Venice. The eldest teaches philosophy at the University of San Diego in California. Ernesto and his family have definitely made great strides forward. The crêpe-soled shoes which drowned in the floodwaters have turned into seven-league boots.

~

Our second restaurateur answered to the name of Nerone. His establishment, Antica Bessetta, was recommended by friends. We would never have come across it otherwise because we didn't stroll around that part of Venice – the Santa Croce *sestiere*, which is only separated by the unattractive Papadopoli Gardens from the Piazzale Roma and the world of cars, noise and commotion. By contrast, the eastern section of this quarter is very peaceful and deserted, but we rarely went over the bridge which divides the pretty square of San Giacomo dell'Orio from the Salizzada del Giusto, where Nerone held sway. The directions we had been given were precise enough for us not to ask for any additional instructions and confusing enough to make us lose our way. Instead of walking towards the Riva di Biasio, very close to the railway station, we headed off towards San Biagio, which is not far from the Arsenal, at the diametrically opposite end of the city. We turned right round and, too inexperienced to know that a boat is not necessarily the most speedy means of locomotion for getting to one's destination, took the vaporetto, which carried us the whole length of the Grand Canal and deposited us on the pontoon of the Riva. After twisting and turning through dark, silent and utterly deserted alleyways, we saw the sign of the trattoria. The entrance led to a large room furnished with a bar and some stools, which was usually empty. The action, except when the restaurant was crowded, was concentrated in the very unpretentious back room, distinguished by its paper tablecloths and walls covered with paintings. A massive serving-table stood in the middle, on it were large glass jars full of fruits in brandy, some drooping gladioli and a fruit stand containing oranges and bananas.

The proprietor showed us to our table. 'Red or white?' He returned with a bottle of *vin ordinaire*, which he planted in front of us. No question of tasting or smelling, let alone choosing the vintage. He left us to serve coffee at the next table and then returned to stand in front of us, his arms folded across his white apron. He looked like a twin brother of the comic actor Louis de Funès, and like an actor he had the gift of making you think he was speaking a foreign language when he wasn't. For a moment I thought that he was addressing us in French, but in fact he had perfected a simplified Italian for talking to tourists. *'Che facciamo?'* ('What shall we make for you?'), he asked. This was a purely formal question. Chez Nerone there was no menu. He suggested and one accepted. The cooking was entirely Venetian, based on fish, crustaceans and pasta; spaghetti with seafood, subtle and seasoned to perfection, octopus, eel, little grilled soles and crayfish – that was what one ate chez Nerone and that was what his wife Maruccia prepared in the large kitchen which opened onto the restaurant. It was utterly simple and it was perfect. 'Everything is fresh here', he said with pride. 'I throw yesterday's fish to the cats.' That made me laugh, because actually one never saw cats scavenging in the Salizzada del Giusto nor in the alley which crossed it, the Ruga del Sagio. This was rare in a city where the smallest square has its cat, or sometimes two, living in little boxes set one on top of the other – this city where caterwauling and bells kept one awake until new European regulations enforced the expulsion of stray cats.

We left delighted and became faithful regulars. We soon became familiar with the itinerary: from the Accademia one simply followed the signs for the railway station as far as San Rocco, then turned diagonally towards the Frari and took the left-hand bridge, being careful not to miss the turning towards the long street which I called Tennis Road, because the netting surmounting its high wall was reminiscent of a court. We then emerged into the irregular square of San Giacomo dell'Orio with its lovely Byzantine church. All that remained was to throw an admiring glance at the neighbouring house with its jasmine-covered terrace and a smile at the noisy young people sitting under the umbrellas of the pizzeria and to cross one last bridge – and we were there. As I have said, we are by nature faithful, but Nerone did not believe in the intrinsic constancy of his regular customers and had perfected an infallible system for ensuring their return. When the time came to pay, he became more like Louis de Funès than ever, all grimaces and gesticulation: 'No, no money, pay me tomorrow. No question, dear sir, oh no, you and I are not going to start signing things. You will take a little grappa before you go.' Only when we were leaving Venice did he finally, after a show of searching in the pocket of his apron, produce a scrap of paper with some figures scrawled on it and announce a total, which of course we could not possibly dispute.

During the week the restaurant was quiet and Nerone managed on his own, certainly running about a lot but so organised and authoritarian (after all, one only ate what he had decided one should eat) that he never gave the impression of being overwhelmed. On Friday and Saturday the two rooms were full and his son Daniele, a good-looking, serious and slightly shy boy, accompanied by some of his fellow medical students from Padua, was there to help out. Nerone did not allow them to take the orders, they just served and cleared the tables.

On the evening before the *riposo settimana*, Maruccia emerged from her kitchen. Her lovely face was prematurely aged, her hands were worn and you could tell from the way she moved how tired her legs were. She sat quietly beside her husband with a glass of water at the table where we were drinking a final grappa, and spoke to us slowly in Italian with the gentleness of someone who does not believe that the person they are talking to will necessarily understand them. However, we noticed that instead of using *lei*, the standard polite form of address, she used *voi*, the older form, which had been brought back into use under Fascism. Nerone continually interrupted her but she paid no attention and went on talking, usually about this only son, the first member of the family to venture out of Venice. Nerone and Maruccia never left their quarter. Sometimes Nerone did go to the Rialto market and sometimes the market-gardeners or the fishermen delivered whatever he needed to the door. On Sundays they went together across the bridge to San Giacomo dell'Orio, which in a way was their town centre. There, little Daniele had spent all his afternoons after school in the church day-care centre. They never let him go about on his own, however tired or busy they were. While Ernesto's gaze was fixed beyond Venice and his curiosity led him to interrogate his customers intelligently about their cities and about world politics – talking music with Raina Kabavanska, the great Bulgarian singer, theatre with Silvano Bussotti and cinema with Mauro Bolognini – Nerone, on the contrary, was anchored in his *sestiere* of Santa Croce. He was born there and had once, only once, been to Saint Mark's – I think without Maruccia. He was a relic of a very ancient tradition from the time when the parishes took pride in their independence and had their *capi di contrade* (local elders), whose influence was demonstrated by the fact that they were summoned daily to the Council of Ten, who wanted to find out what was going on. Most often what was going on was a massive brawl, because the quarrels and rivalry between the parishes were settled with fisticuffs, those *battaglie di pugni* which made an irresistible spectacle for nobles, populace and visitors alike.

Daniele finished his medical studies, worked for a spell in the United States, came back to settle in Venice and got married. Was Maruccia happy about this turn of events? She showed little enthusiasm. Her daughter-in-law, a paediatrician, always seemed to be rushing about, she said, always on the telephone, always under pressure. The young couple just grabbed a hurried bite to eat except when they came to the restaurant. They were going to ruin their stomachs, going on like this. And no baby on the horizon. 'How are they going to produce a child with all this stress?' she wondered. 'Stress' has in fact no equivalent in Italian; it was the only foreign word I ever heard Maruccia use. The dark rings under her eyes became deeper every year. One evening Nerone told us that Daniele was worried. There was something the matter with her stomach. A niece came to help her and to Nerone's great relief Maruccia taught her all her secrets, but we never learnt the end of the story. When we returned the following autumn, Nerone had sold the restaurant.

That's when we moved to Mara and Maurizio's.

~

During the years when we dined chez Nerone, we would go to the restaurant quickly, by the shortest itinerary, because we were always late. It is tiresome to have to stop writing when one has got into a good rhythm; one wants to follow through one's train of thought and finish the paragraph.

One of the reasons why we avoid invitations and appointments is precisely because we refuse to restrict ourselves to fixed hours. However, Venice is not Seville and one cannot decently prolong the evening too far before dining. We would compensate by wandering aimlessly though the streets on the way home, continually changing our itinerary, sometimes taking a vaporetto for the pleasure of seeing the great façades of palaces on both sides of the Grand Canal illuminated by the moon and sometimes making a wide detour to emerge into Saint Mark's Square – deserted at last. If we decided to go through San Polo, one of the great *campi* of Venice where lovely palaces with inward curving façades evoke the memory of the vanished canal on which they used to stand, and which seems all the more peaceful at night because by then the little football players and apprentice tricyclists who occupy it by day are in bed, we would pass along a street where a swaying lantern decorated with a flower marked the entrance to what looked like one of those wine bars where one drinks *un'ombra* accompanied by a tidbit, a *cichetto*. The place was called, of course, Da Fiore. We learnt that it was in fact a restaurant, but the dining-room was invisible from the street. When we asked the concierge at our hotel to make a reservation for us, he said unenthusiastically, 'Oh, I'll try but I can't promise. They are always full.' Show us an obstacle and we insist on surmounting it. 'Please try hard, if not for this evening, then for tomorrow or another day. It doesn't matter when.' Finally we got what we wanted.

It was raining hard that evening and my husband was suffering from sciatica. I suggested cancelling this precious reservation. Why run around the streets and over the bridges instead of just crossing our piazza and going to Ernesto's? A lesser mortal would have indeed stayed home, but I was dealing with a man of principle: 'It has been difficult enough to get this reservation and we cannot let them down at the last minute. It wouldn't be right.' His only concession was to take the vaporetto across the Grand Canal instead of hobbling all the way.

Naturally we arrived late and soaked through as well. It isn't easy to walk around Venice under an umbrella; most of the time you can't open it in the very narrow passageways, where Goethe said you could touch both sides by putting your hands on your hips. At Da Fiore you go through the bar, push open a glass door and find yourself in the first room, which adjoins the kitchen (seen through a large serving-hatch) and holds a set of shelves full of handsome carafes and a table for the essential items of equipment for running a business – telephone, fax and a large cash register. On hearing our name, the proprietor opened his ledger and announced that our reservation was in fact for the following day but, being a humane man, he relented when confronted with our disappointed faces and my wet feet. The rush had subsided and tables were emptying. After conferring briefly with the kitchen, he turned to us. 'Come along, it will be all right; come and sit down.' We entered the restaurant proper – a long and very attractive room with light-coloured walls and no windows. There were flowers on every table, around which replete customers seemed to be purring with satisfaction.

The restaurateur was Maurizio, a good-looking man with regular features and hair just long enough to make him look casual, although he never relaxed. His eyes were everywhere. In his dark suit and Ferragamo tie, whether boning a fish or filling empty glasses with rapid, precise movements, he was ceaselessly directing his troops – three or four black-clad waiters, always on the move. It was a very elegant place, more like the Gritti or the Monaco than the back room of a wine bar in San Polo. When we met him, Maurizio only spoke Italian, but a very pretty young girl was given the task of receiving foreigners and advising them on the food. Obviously she spoke English, but she also spoke Japanese – proof that Da Fiore counted on an international clientele. She, too, was very elegant, dressed in a simple black dress and, like her employer, courteous without being obsequious and endlessly patient. Nothing is more irritating than having to translate a menu, particularly a fish menu, since the species vary from sea to sea: is a branzino a sea bass or a dogfish? No idea!

Maurizio gave my husband the wine list but at his request remained at his side. Louis has often told me how much he regrets that it is impossible to taste every vintage, but long sojourns in France have given him the opportunity of filling a number of gaps. His knowledge, however, did not extend to Italian wines, the production of which has changed considerably in recent years. One or two generations ago these remarkable wines were practically unknown outside Italy. In the sixties the mention of Italian wine conjured up the image of Chianti in straw-covered bottles. Since then the progress in viniculture techniques has improved the quality and longevity of these wines which are of a dizzying variety and diversity, there being in Italy over 400 types of vine, infinite variations in the soil, micro-climates and a wide range of skill among the cultivators. So the choice is difficult, if one rejects the easy option of being guided by price. You have to know how to decipher the label and to take into account the type of grape, the vineyard and the producer's reputation – something you cannot learn in a fortnight. Ernesto had guided us through the realms of red wines and introduced us to those of the Friuli and the Alto Adige as well as the Veneto. Sometimes he would uncork a great Chianti, sometimes a Dolcetto, and sometimes he would invite us to compare the different years of Vistorta wines. At Da Fiore, thanks to Maurizio, we discovered the charms of white wines and also food of exceptional quality. Chez Nerone, the fare was excellent but a little rustic; chez Maurizio, simplicity reached its pinnacle. We were ready to be adopted and we were. Until the end of our stay he gave us a table every time we asked for one, preferably after 9 pm.

Maurizio's wife, the beautiful Mara, was the artist who fried small fish to filigree lightness, cooked black pasta with squid with a hint of lemon to bring out the flavour, fish with firm or soft flesh and a fluffy, bitter chocolate soufflé. At closing time you would see her sitting at the bar, a slightly plump, dark-haired woman, always smiling, with merry, friendly eyes. When we had got to know her a little, she kissed me when I told her that my *stomacchino e contentissimo.* 'You are not too tired?' I asked her as we left? 'No', she said, laughing, 'Maurizio has the difficult job; he has to deal with the customers. In the kitchen everyone does what I tell them.' They had been working together for a long time, for they were still in their teens and already the parents of a little boy, Damiano, when they borrowed the money to open a *baccaro*, one of those typical Venetian bars which serve miniscule hors-d'oeuvres – tiny mouthfuls of a variety of food served on saucers to go with a glass of wine. It lay in an undistinguished quarter between San Polo and San Giacomo dell'Orio, at that time little frequented by tourists, where their clientele consisted of artisans, house painters, carpenters, picture-framers and representatives of all the little trades of Venice. The food was so good that very soon everyone lingered on and ended up eating a real meal. Mara began by offering a *plat du jour*, but gradually the menu grew. Her reputation spread through the quarter and business went well enough for Maurizio to decide to expand and open a proper restaurant.

Maurizio had a good head for business. He had set his sights beyond Venice or rather, he understood that in the eighties success, brilliant success (he was ambitious) required one to come out of one's shell. A trattoria was all right but a quality restaurant was better. One had to go up-market — no paper tablecloths, not even checked ones, no apron-clad proprietor, no waiters in shirtsleeves, no local colour, but still pure, typical Venetian cooking. The young couple's friendship with Marcella Hazan, one of the doyennes of Italian cooking in the USA, was a great help. Copies of her cookery books sell in hundreds of thousands and if you want to attend one of her cookery courses, you have to wait two or three years and pay $3000 for a week's tuition. For a long time she divided her life among Venice, Bologna and Chicago, but now she has retired and settled in Florida with her husband. Marcella recognised Mara's talents immediately; she introduced her to editors of magazines, which printed her recipes in their columns and so opened for her the door to the American food business. Da Fiore was mentioned

47

in more and more guidebooks, but the definitive break-through came in 1994, when Patricia Wells, the gastronomic correspondent of the *Herald Tribune*, included it in her list of the ten best restaurants in the world. We read the article in the aeroplane from Paris to Venice and on our arrival, our first visit being – as always – to Ernesto's, we broke the news to him.

Ernesto usually judged his colleagues severely. He would say that the food they served was downright bad and might add 'Anyhow, that's not surprising: at lunchtime all these tourists are in a hurry and in the evening they stay away. In the daytime you can't get across the Accademia Bridge and at night Venice is empty, *vuota*. There are not enough people to make up a clientele. Or else' – and his voice would become even more contemptuous – 'they don't know about Venetian traditions.' He admitted that Mara was a very good cook but 'One of the best in the world?

Come on! What is that supposed to mean?' He was not moved by jealousy or bitterness; he simply did not understand this hyperbole, which seemed to him ridiculous, if not despicable. To him cooking was a game, *un gioco;* it had to be simple and enjoyable, for friends gathering together around a table. One should not make a drama out of it.

However, nothing had changed at Da Fiore. The welcome was just as warm and the enquiries about our children just as attentive. Since I had never seen the room except when it was full, the atmosphere did not seem to me to have changed. As usual, there were plenty of foreigners but the Venetian clientele was still there — that clientele whose presence guaranteed the purity of the cuisine. Maurizio had made some alterations, changing the lighting and trying to improve the acoustic (he hated noise) and was preparing to make a hole through the back wall in order to open a window onto the canal. But, yes, there was something new: he addressed us in English. 'What has happened? Berlitz?' we asked. 'No', he laughed, 'I went on a crash course in Ireland for six weeks. Yes, I did learn some words, but at what a price! What weather! What appalling food! Only the salmon was edible but eating salmon every evening – what a night-mare!' He had also sent his son as an apprentice to a great Italian restaurant in New York. He wanted the young man to learn his trade – and English.

Maurizio knew how to make a grand gesture. On our last evening, when it came to paying, the waiter told us that we had been the guests of the house. We had often been offered a brandy by a restaurateur, or perhaps a bottle of wine to apologise for a delay, but a whole meal, and such a splendid meal – never! Embarrassed and touched, we did not know how to thank him, until he said he would be in New York during the winter. We made him promise to telephone. In fact he sent a fax to announce his arrival and we arranged to take him out to lunch. We opted for our favourite French restaurant, renowned for its cuisine and its flowers. Maurizio arrived punctually. After being introduced to the proprietor and having cast a quick look around the restaurant, which seemed to satisfy him, he took out his mobile phone with an apology. The evening was beginning in Venice and he wanted to make sure all was going well at Da Fiore. He was not worried about the cooking but Damiano, who had been working with his parents since his return, lacked experience. We listened to Maurizio running his restaurant from 5000 kilometres away, suggesting what wine to recommend for the table round which eight dentists on a congress had just gathered and advising Damiano to persuade a honeymoon couple to wait at the bar with a glass of *prosecco*. When he had finished, he confessed that he was not at all hungry. 'One eats too much in New York', he murmured. Perhaps he was just dreaming of his fish ravioli.

That was not our last meal together. The following year, on the evening of our arrival in Venice, he was sitting with us over coffee and, at the risk of causing a revolt among American diners, encouraged us to light a cigarillo and took one himself. 'Shall we go out together next Sunday?' he asked with a big smile. We, who are usually so firm in refusing any commitment of this kind, found ourselves disarmed by his kindness and, moreover, curious to know where he would take us, so we accepted with a good grace. Two days later, he asked us whether we would mind his inviting some acquaintances, an American couple of Italian origin, whom he had known since he started in business. 'Not at all', we said, 'of course not', all the more because that might make conversation easier. He asked us to meet him in front of the Giardinetti, at the landing-stage for the Cipriani boat. 'Too bad!' said Louis to me. We were not going to discover hidden treasure, we were going straight to the competition, the competition being Cipriani, the luxury hotel with countless stars in the guidebooks, nestling on Giudecca Island – a place we considered extremely pretentious. But it was too late to back out.

At the appointed hour we met Mara and Maurizio, both madly chic, she in a black and white Missoni dress with a pretty bag on her arm and he in linen trousers and a pale suede blouson, soft as butter – arm in arm, happy and carefree like a pair of lovers. Then the two Americans made their appearance. The man, whose crumpled clothes looked as though they had just come out of a suitcase, was a head taller than any of us although he stooped, while the woman trotting at his side, poured into a black, multicoloured print dress, was a grotesquely fat dwarf. 'Signor Ladrone, Signor Begley', said Maurizio and I bit my lip to stop bursting out laughing and lowered my eyes so as not to meet Louis's gaze. We, the unsociable misanthropists, were going to step into a boat with Ladrones – 'robbers' from a little town in Rhode Island? The mafia couldn't be far away.

We took our seats in the launch to the Giudecca, where Cipriani's had recently opened a restaurant with an open-air annexe on a floating pontoon over the canal, which is very wide at this point, but no sooner had we sat down at table than the sky clouded over, the first raindrops fell and we had to take refuge inside. Maurizio took charge and ordered for everyone, while Mara told me the story of her early life, her apprenticeship under the tutelage of her grandmother, an excellent cook who had only prepared meals for her family. ('You see, there were a lot of us', explained Mara.) She told me that a chef's work above all requires perpetual discipline and then delightedly described their house on *terra firma*. It sometimes seems to me that the Venetians have only one idea: to escape from the bridges and canals in search of roads and cars. Over dessert she suggested we should call each other '*tu*'. I enthusiastically accepted this friendly proposal, although my rudimentary Italian was very formal. I knew how to use the polite form of address but I found the familiar form very difficult. Meanwhile the Ladrones revealed that they were not gangsters but owners of a thriving insurance agency. They were especially knowledgeable about health claims. At the time that was not yet a subject dear to our hearts. Maurizio, always on the alert, was studying the restaurant and the service and made some rapid comments to his wife in Venetian dialect. When the dessert came, he rose and settled the bill discreetly. It only remained to thank him diplomatically: 'What a marvellous evening', Louis said to him, 'but really the food was nothing like Mara's and tomorrow we shall be happy to resume our usual routine at your place.' This formula gave Maurizio great satisfaction.

In the US you have not been awarded the final culinary accolade until you have published a book.

Nearly a thousand cookery books come out every year. There is a bookshop in New York which specialises in them and the branches of chains like Barnes and Nobles and Borders have whole shelves devoted to the mysteries of roasting and braising. Of course Da Fiore was featured in all the guides and gastronomic articles about Venice, Marcella Hazan's course on Venetian cooking ended with lunch at the restaurant and Mara's recipes appeared regularly in magazines. However, they could do better, and in the spring of 2002 Maurizio gave us the great news at once: 'It has happened! Damiano has finally signed a contract to write the Da Fiore cookbook.' What a triumph! The book was to come out shortly. We confirmed that the publication should be appropriately celebrated – with a big party at our home in New York. We then attacked our *frittura mista*.

But Maurizio had another surprise for us. Damiano had set up on his own and opened a pizzeria a few steps away at San Giacomo dell'Orio. 'You must go there', he said, 'you will see how delightful it is.' Our friendship with Maurizio led us to do the strangest things: to dine with Ladrones at Cipriani and to eat a pizza in Venice. However, we did not regret our excursion to Damiano's. He had taken over the place we passed on our way to Nerone's, but what a transformation! Pretty seats in place of the white plastic chairs which seem to have covered pavements the whole world over, Rothko posters on the walls, sprightly waitresses and stylish customers. Damiano, whom I had only ever seen dressed to kill in a suit, gaily did the honours at La Rafale in a navy polo-neck shirt and trainers. His pizzas were very good and he recommended an orange *bavaroise* to follow. 'It is my mother's recipe.' How could we refuse? When we came to pay he absolutely refused to give us a bill. 'This is your first visit to my restaurant', he said. 'You are my guests.' There is a Venetian tradition which is not often mentioned in front of foreigners, the *voce amica* – a little gift, a discount of about ten per cent, which restaurateurs bestow on their fellow-citizens. We had received our formal naturalisation. Not just one 'voice', but a whole chorus of friend-ship, seemed to welcome us into our adopted city.

Ernesto, Nerone and Maurizio provided the framework for our evenings. At lunchtime we went to Harry's Dolci, where tables were set out on the quay of the Giudecca once the good weather started. In spite of what its name suggests, the Giudecca was never a Jewish quarter; the term comes from the *giudicati* or the condemned, because insurgents were banished to this island in the 9th century. In fact there is still a prison on Giudecca, but except for its inmates the place – part of Venice and yet outside it – is magical, one of those rare spots from which to view the panorama of the city as it appears on postcards of the canals, where the artist has taken the trouble to paint in all the façades. The canal of the Giudecca is wide enough to allow one to take in the whole southern panorama of Venice, from the San Sebastiano Canal, beyond which one can see the parked cars and trucks, as far as the bend which leads to the Customs House. Yet one is near enough to distinguish the passers-by on the other side of the canal, very small in the distance but lively and clear like the figures in Guardi's paintings. One year the Venice marathon was on offer, as well. Planks had been laid over the steps of all the bridges so as not to break the runners' rhythm. From the distance one did not sense their efforts but only saw the different styles of the competitors.

Another marvel was how difficult it was to identify the different church and bell towers rising behind the first line of houses. As always in Venice, changing one's position seems to change all the distances, too. For instance, a church one was accustomed to approaching from the front (like San Zaccaria, for example) assumed surprising dimensions when seen from afar. It was a puzzle to put names to the various buildings. There were plenty of other distractions to occupy one's mealtimes: watching the big cruise ships moored or being pulled by tugs, the course of the various ferries loaded with cars and passengers en route for the Lido or the unloading of barges bringing boxes of food to the supermarket which had just opened opposite on the Zattere. One suddenly realised why all commodities in the city are so expensive: the smallest delivery requires so much time and effort. Finally the coming and going of the very varied boats on the Canal, each loaded, as the case might be, with bricks, planks, barrels, a mountain of melons, a washing machine or a cooker, made a constantly changing spectacle. On the occasion of the *vola longa*, that incomprehensible race in which both the fastest rowing boats with eight oars and the most primitive craft take part, the activity became all the more frenetic, because the large boat club was on the opposite shore. And finally, the relative difficulty of getting to the Dolci gave our mornings a particular flavour.

For me one of the charms of Venice is the perpetual problem it gives the pedestrian: there is never just one way to get from A to B in the city; there are always two or three. In any other town the signs are clear: right, left or straight ahead. In Venice no such simplicity applies. It does not matter whether you turn right or left, you will reach your destination. The important thing is choosing your itinerary. Therefore, as we lived near the Fenice, we had to cross the Grand Canal and then the Giudecca Canal to get to our lunch. Such a range of choice opened up to us! To go to Saint Mark's and take a direct boat to the Giudecca, as our concierge recommended, seemed too easy; we preferred to cross the Accademia bridge or take the gondola *traghetto* which plies between the two banks from Santa Maria del Giglio towards the Salute every five minutes (except when the gondoliers go to have a drink, eat their lunch or take a siesta), unless we decided to take the traghetto at the Palazzo Grassi. You then walk swiftly over Dorsoduro from the Accademia to the Gesuati on the Zattere and then a thorny problem arises: how to cross the Giudecca Canal. The first time we went to the Dolci we were so ignorant that we thought the restaurant would send a motor launch, Cipriani-style, to collect its customers and we waited patiently until a passer-by disabused us. It was necessary to take a vaporetto, unless you had come in a gondola or a taxi motorboat. But which vaporetto? For a long time one of them went back and forth (*faceva traghetto*) making this simple, but then the service was discontinued. The normal vaporetti going down the length of the canal either stop or don't stop at Santa Eufemia, the nearest halt to the Dolci. The distances are so short that this is not in the least important but the mysterious principle underlying it bothered us. For the last two or three years the landing-stages have given the precise itineraries and timetables and, oddly enough, the Venetian vaporetti are as reliable as Swiss trains. But in a less well-organised past we lived in a perpetual state of uncertainty.

When our morning walks took us farther, towards the Madonna dell Orto or the Gesuiti (the home of Titian's great *Martyrdom of St Lawrence)* or the church of Santi Giovanni e Polo, we often took the *giracittà* – the vaporetto which goes right round the city. Going west towards the railway station, its route takes you beyond Canareggio and the station towards the industrial zone. Once the port of Venice was in front of the Doge's Palace, but today it has slipped down the length of the Giudecca Canal to the extreme south of Dorsoduro. This commercial port was not a place to walk to, and from the bridge of the vaporetto it was amazing to see a group of modern moles, quays and warehouses so close to the city. We sailed past railway lines where empty goods wagons stood and in the distance saw the smoking factory chimneys of Marghera – a whole world away from our Venice, which we regained with relief when the boat had passed the headland of Sacco Santa Marta and far away in the sunlit haze we saw the glitter of golden cupolas. However, when we took the *giracittà* in the opposite direction, our chosen itinerary went nobly past the Arsenal until a reconstruction programme barred the way. Later, when the work was in progress, the *giracittà* was forced to make an enormous loop towards the Lido and past the unknown world of the Castello, the Stadium and the Botanical Gardens before rejoining the basin of Saint Mark's. Our self-imposed commitment to arriving at the Giudecca at around two o'clock every day – otherwise lunch, and therefore the afternoon's work, would be delayed excessively – involved us in some unexpected journeys.

Harry's Dolci served mixed Italian and international cuisine simultaneously. One could keep to Venetian food and order a risotto with black squid or a *baccalà* (a brandade of salt cod), ignore local colour and choose a club sandwich, just make one's meal out of a huge chef's salad, or indeed succumb to the sinful delights of a range of irresistible desserts – lemon meringue pie, a zabaglione gateau filled with whipped cream, a chocolate tart or ices and sorbets of every hue. The presiding genius and master of ceremonies at Harry's Dolci, Signor Bruno, was exquisitely urbane and accommodated all culinary tastes with an impassive smile. He was not one of the race of restaurateurs; he was a *maître d'hôtel*. While our other three hosts were chatty and extrovert, Signor Bruno insisted on maintaining a façade of completely professional dignity to go with his black suit which, closely fitting at the waist, made him look like a wasp, and which was sometimes enlivened with a brightly-coloured tie.

And like a giant wasp he pursued the sparrows who came to peck from the plates.

As a result we knew nothing about him. Was he married? Did he live in Venice? Where had he learnt his perfect English and his impeccable French? He did not invite questions but instead enjoyed giving us a detailed account of the triumphs of the Cipriani dynasty. Harry's Dolci was a branch of the famous Harry's Bar, founded in 1931 by Giuseppe Cipriani in an alley leading into Saint Mark's Basin. Bar? Restaurant? How should one define this place? It had become a Venetian institution, the birthplace of *bellini* (purée of white peaches mixed with *prosecco*), and of *carpaccio*, which consists of transparently thin slices of raw beef, served with a hint of mayonnaise and a sliver of lemon – a dish which seems to have conquered the western world, while *bellini* is impossible to reproduce. So many famous people have passed through the bar – writers like Hemingway who featured it in his novel *Across the River and into the Trees*, actors (they tell how Orson Welles always ordered two bottles of Dom Pérignon to wash down his meal), singers (Callas, followed by her cohort of admirers, came here every time she was passing through) and the stars of the Venice Festival – that the barman and the waiters, a little blasé, did not abandon their regular customers to pay court to the celebrities of the day, which gave the place a curiously cosy and unaffected atmosphere.

Giuseppe's son, Arrigo, had built up the business, opening first Harry's Dolci on the Giudecca and then the Locanda Cipriani on the island of Torcello – an exquisitely peaceful spot, so perfect for writing that every year we were tempted to stay there. But paradoxically, the Cipriani Hotel did not belong to him. Arrigo next turned his eyes towards America and established a forward base in Argentina, from which he set out to conquer New York, a goal he accomplished, ruling over two restaurants, a banqueting hall and the Rainbow

Room, an Art Deco ballroom and dining room at the top of the Rockefeller Center. To maintain the quality of the *bellini* the peach purée had to be frozen in Italy, because American peaches do not have the same flavour. Bruno joined in his employer's international glory to the extent of spending his winters at the Rockefeller Center in New York, but he was not a man to enter into the details of his daily life. We did not know how he lived in either Venice or New York, nor even whether he liked the latter.

For gastronomic reasons our relations did become a little more personal. One day, when Louis lamented the absence of white asparagus from the menu, Bruno's face lit up: 'Tomorrow we are closed. I am going to see my aunt who has a garden on the *terra firma*. She grows the best asparagus in the region and I shall bring some back for you.' In fact it was exquisite and Bruno served us with some every day until the end of our visit. Emboldened, we confessed to our great liking for tripe, which is a very popular dish in Italy, served in very different ways according to the region, but did not seem appropriate for this establishment, where the menu was restricted to a classicism as elegant as it was cautious. Bruno evinced a surprising enthusiasm when we made this tentative remark. 'Wait, I shall go and talk to the *laboratorio*.' This meant the kitchen which, curiously enough, was not next to the restaurant but two doors down the street. On rainy days one could see the waiters emerging with dishes covered with great bells of plastic. They got soaking wet but the food was safeguarded. Bruno came back beaming: the chef would be delighted to cook it for us 'but', he said, 'at the weekend. He will have to make a large quantity and the Italian customers mostly come on Saturdays and Sundays. Foreigners are suspicious of tripe.'

It was true that during the week the clientele did in fact mainly consist of English or French tourists who seemed to be regulars like us, but from

Saturday lunchtime on the atmosphere changed. The parties were larger and grandparents came with their whole families. Sometimes a wedding breakfast involved rearranging the whole terrace; no one objected because by tradition the bride distributed pieces of cake to all the customers. Italian was the main language. The tripe was a triumph, delicate, subtle and flavoured with a little parmesan. Bruno watched us out of the corner of his eye, smiling, sure that he had pulled it off. 'Ours are not the usual tripe, they are calves' tripe, hence their unparalleled lightness.' The cook had gone to town and we ate tripe for lunch on Saturday, Sunday and Monday. At the end of the third meal the staff came to thank us: as there was some left over, and the restaurant was closed on Tuesdays, the personnel were going to eat it for their dinner. Ever since, on the first day of our vacation, Bruno greeted us with '*Buon giorno!* Shall we have tripe on Saturday?' The waiters went into action and brought us a small carafe of red wine before we had even opened the menu. Our transition into the next sphere of regulars was ratified with the *voce amica* when the bill came. Who would have thought that one of the keys to open for us the door to this mysterious city would assume the form of a dish of tripe with parsley.

And then, suddenly, Bruno disappeared. A young man dressed exactly like him with a lovely Tintoretto face was officiating in his place when we came back in 2001. He had been well coached and immediately suggested preparing tripe for us the following Saturday. 'Bruno is resting', he said. 'He has just come back from New York and has not started work again.' The following year there was still no Bruno and this time the young man explained that Cipriani had opened a café in Grand Central Station in New York, where Bruno was working. I was so sad to think of Bruno in that great hall, even though it had recently been renovated and was very beautiful and monumental, that I decided to pay him a visit. But no Bruno. No one knew who I was talking about.

Finally, one of our New York friends who, like us, knew Venice well, announced that he had found Bruno again, not in a Cipriani restaurant but working for another Italian dynasty, the Maccionis. Father Maccioni ran a restaurant called the Cirque, which had enjoyed a great reputation for more than a quarter of a century. He had given his sons a jollier, more modern restaurant, to manage – L'Osteria del Circo – and had engaged Bruno, whom he had known for a long time, to keep an eye on it. We went there that very evening and were greeted warmly by our dear Bruno, who hastened off to fetch us a carafe of red wine and some sparkling water without our having to ask. He then left us for a moment to make sure that the kitchen could still serve tripe. When he returned, we told him how much we had missed him. What had happened? Discreet as always, Bruno did not go into details. He had trained Antonio but there was no room for both of them at the Dolci and after the events of 9/11 things had not gone well in the Rainbow Room. The skyscrapers had lost their charm. So he had come back to Maccioni. We then learnt that as a young man he had served his apprenticeship at Harry's Bar and then went to England. Having learnt English, he set sail for New York, where he stayed for 12 years at the Cirque before returning to Venice and Cipriani. Now he was once again dividing his time between New York and Venice, where he lived with his wife and daughter. The wheel had come full circle for Bruno, but also for us. This was a man, personifying for us a certain style and *joie de vivre* which were peculiarly Venetian, unchanged and now settled in one of the most lively quarters of our city.

Of course our Venice, with its centuries-old façades bathed in the sea-green waters of the canals, our Venice resounding with the cries of birds, with bells and with the sound of our feet in the deserted alleyways, our mysterious and unique Venice, of which we dreamt all year round, cannot be transplanted. But how could one overlook the fact that at least the more ambitious of its inhabitants dream of America? All our Venetian-born friends had either themselves, or by proxy through a son or daughter, set foot on the other side of the Atlantic. Ernesto's daughter was doing well in California, Nerone's son had studied in the States, Mara, Maurizio and Damiano had ensured their success by spreading their tentacles to Florida and New York and now Bruno, approaching the obligatory retirement age in Italy, seemed determined to continue his career in Manhattan. How could we deny that if Venice's charm had drawn us to it so faithfully for nearly a quarter of a century, it was because, over and above its ancient beauties, the talent, the energy and the enterprising spirit of our Venetian friends had kept our curiosity alive?

The Only Way
to
Enter Venice

by Louis Begley

The only way to enter Venice, said Lilly, is in a gondola. Anything else is a sacrilege. If you take a gondola from the train station to your hotel, in my opinion you will have done justice to the city and to yourself. I should tell you that no less an authority than Thomas Mann disagrees. Anyway he disagreed when he wrote *Death in Venice*. He wrote there that to arrive in Venice by train is like entering a palace through a back door. He thought you must arrive by ship, across the open sea, so that the palace of the Doges, the Bridge of Sighs, and the columns supporting the winged lion and St. Theodore will rise up before you - magically. I wonder whether he still thinks so today, when you just don't go to Venice by ship unless you like cruise boats and travel in organized groups.

At the time, I had not read Mann's novella, although *The Magic Mountain* was one of my favorite novels. I had read it during the summer after my graduation from high school. It was my intention to major in history, and I had it firmly in mind that I would become a military historian. An English teacher who knew about my interest in World War I and the long prelude to it that started with the battle of Sadowa said that Mann's novel would be right up my alley. She couldn't have been more right. Now I was about to graduate from Harvard College and my passion for military history had not weakened. When I confessed my ignorance to Lilly, she laughed and said, how lucky you are. You have two great treats ahead of you. The first experience of Venice and of *Death in Venice.* Both of us laughed at the pun. I will give you the Mann to read on the train, she continued. You can do it on the night train from Paris to Venice. I assume you will not pay for a *couchette* so you won't sleep that night anyway. The train station is right on the Grand Canal. Gondolas will be waiting. You will give your suitcase to the gondoliere, tell him the name of your hotel or, better yet, give him the name and address on a piece of paper, and lie back like a king in the red plush seat. But please make sure your eyes stay open. The most beautiful spectacle in the world, a fairyland of Gothic architecture, will glide past you. Unfortunately, by the time you realize that you would like the ride to go on forever, it will be over. The gondola will have stopped next to some slippery stone steps overgrown with algae that are a break in the *rio* running along that segment of the side canal. Your hotel will be meters away.

That is how Lilly talked – like a book. Of course, she didn't think for a moment that she needed to introduce the famous German novelist into our conversation for her words to have authority. She was just acting out her role of the daughter of the chairman of the English department at Harvard, a cantankerous personage who had been teaching his great course on Chaucer to undergraduates longer than any living man could remember – some claimed he had been at it since the time of Chaucer – as well as those of the muse and mostly anonymous patroness of the Poets' Theater, and my own cultural and social *cicerone*. The fact is that I accepted blindly the worldly advice and reproofs with which she was so generous, no matter how bitter I sometimes found their taste. There wasn't an aspect of my person or conduct too trivial for her attention and comments, and I was convinced it was all for my good. I won't say that she put my mother to shame – the poor woman had surely done her best, even with my three younger sisters and my father, lurching from one bout of depression to another, to lay claims to her attention. But no one had ever examined me so closely or put down so many rules for my conduct as Lilly. They aimed variously at my diction, table manners and clothes, and the lacunae in my knowledge of literature, art and music. In my mind, the open question was only whether in the murky future I would attain the enhanced level of existence for which they were intended. Besides, I was in love with Lilly – and with all the things she had that I did not, and until recently had not imagined myself within reach of possessing.

I was also obsessed by her body, although so far I had not managed to go beyond kissing her on the mouth, with our tongues in busy communion, sucking the nipples of her breasts, which she did not always allow, caressing the insides of her thighs, and on certain rare occasions, when she had drunk more whiskey after dinner than usual, kneading, through her panties, her mons veneris and labia. As she wore the old-fashioned kind, that covered, in addition to the usual territory, two or three inches of her thighs, foraging inside them was impractical unless it was to be undertaken from the waist down, and that was an initiative that nothing had until that time encouraged me to dare. I had not seen her mons, because of those panties, but I imagined it soft as corn silk and curly, like the head of a baby angel, except that Lilly's hair was black. There was a mixture of beauty and imperfection that, quite literally, made me faint, in her mouth, with its lips that were beautifully formed and teeth that stuck out just a little and felt almost jagged and sharp on my tongue, her breasts that were covered with a milky way of freckles, and her thighs. The thighs deserve special mention: they were heavy, which didn't repel me at all, very strong because she was an expert horsewoman, and, toward the end of the cycle between one depilation and another, prickly. I knew that those heavy, prickly thighs were not the attributes of a pinup, and that they embarrassed Lilly. But for me the stubble meant secrecy. When I ran my hand over it, the roughness was another sign that I was in the precincts of the holy of holies. The heft of her thighs and her buttocks was an indispensable element of daydreams about how I would mount her.

At twenty, I was young to be graduating. She was seven years older than I, and had gone to Smith. Afterward, she had spent a couple of years in Europe, working as a part-timer first for the *Herald Tribune* and then *Time*. An ugly case of some illness you catch from unpasteurized milk contracted while she was skiing in Zermatt forced her to return to Cambridge. She recovered completely, except for an occasional spell of great fatigue, and had a morning job in the office of the dean in charge of scholarships, where I was a frequent visitor, frequent enough to have dared to invite her for coffee. My business there had to do with the university scholarship that made it possible for me to go to Harvard College in the first place, and, more recently, with the fellowship I had been awarded for two years' study in Europe after graduation. It was the stipend connected with that fellowship that was going to finance a summer of travel in Europe, where I had never been. Venice became my first destination when Lilly told me, in a voice that whatever my hand was doing to her labia had made languorous, that she would be there toward the end of June. Perhaps we could meet, she murmured, I am a good tour guide.

These amatory sessions took place away from my room in the college house and the parietal rules that regulated the presence of women, on a daybed in the living room of her apartment on Memorial Drive. Lilly had money from a trust established by her maternal grandfather, who had been a successful inventor. It gave her the sort of freedom I had never yet observed at close quarters. It came down to this: she did what she wanted, whether it was a matter of renting and furnishing an apartment in that citadel-like building, or buying a little bottle-green convertible because she liked the way it looked and how it went with her hair, or announcing that she would go on a vacation in Europe, or paying for a production by the Poet's Theater of *Six Characters in Search of an Author.* I was generally aware that some people in my college class had very rich families, and I could see the difference that made in the clothes they wore, which were often made by a tailor on Mt. Auburn Street at whose store window I cast furtive and admiring glances, and in their trips at Christmas time to islands in the Caribbean, but I was too distant from them, and from the college clubs at which I imagined such things were discussed among insiders, to understand the difference. Now I was seeing practically at first hand how those who have wealth use it. For a scholarship student from a small town in New Hampshire, these were lessons pregnant with meaning.

I would visit Lilly in the afternoon, around teatime, after she had had her nap, but more usually for dinner. She liked to cook, and made something of a specialty of lamb chops, calf's liver, chicken livers, orzo and spinach. When I could afford it – usually just after I had been paid by the parents of one of the high school students I tutored – I would bring a bottle of wine, hoping it would pass muster with Lilly as not undrinkable or stupidly expensive. At the appropriate time, I would maneuver us to the daybed. Seated on it, we read poetry, chosen by her, which she would ask me to explicate. Little by little, as we bent over the page, my arm would find its way around her waist and my hand would cover her breast. Or I would begin by stroking her legs and her knees. If she didn't push my hand away, I would quickly reach the inside of her thighs. The panderer book would go face down on the coffee table. We could easily spend two hours in this sort of play, interrupted by getting drinks – after dinner, she liked strong scotch whiskey and soda highballs, with ice filling the glass to the brim – changing records on her record player, drinking, and trips to the bathroom occasioned by the ingestion of a great deal of liquid. She was usually passive: eyes shut, letting me caress her. Her only gesture toward me was to take hold of my member and squeeze it, through the layers of my trousers and shorts, as though to test its hardness. She would say that my little man was to be congratulated on his patience. I didn't share her views about the little man; I groaned with the desire to have her hand remain on my penis and give me the signal to come, but when I tried to show her what I wanted, she invariably shook her head and said no, that was not what she intended. It was clear that I had better control myself. Shooting my load into my trousers, as had happened to me often with other girls, could only diminish both my standing and prospects.

I have said that I would maneuver her, and that is how it most seemed to me then, but when I now think about it I am certain that it was the other way around. She was the stage manager of our entertainments. She liked sex without the uncertainties of sex. I knew that once a week, sometimes more often, she had real sex that did not include any of our games with a trust officer who managed her money and had the additional attribute of being the husband of her mother's school friend. This was a relationship she claimed she wanted to stop because, as she put it, the banker used her as a convenience, like a public toilet. There was also an involvement with an Italian aristocrat she wouldn't name, whose family planned a brilliant future for him. I thought that she was in love with him, and that the vacation in Europe, the outline of which beyond the days she planned to spend in Venice she didn't seem to want to disclose, was intended to reestablish contact with the *marchesino*. When I asked whether she wanted to marry him, she answered that she did, but wasn't at all sure that such were his intentions. For one thing, she was an American. That problem could be overcome, and she was even willing to convert. The real difficulty arose from her not being rich enough. His situation required a greater fortune. This information left me perplexed. I had come to the view that Lilly stood at the summit of chic, and she seemed to me to have ample wealth. As she was an only child, it also seemed probable that more money would come to her after the death of her parents.

My own affair with her reached a new plateau — in the low foothills, hardly above the tree line, in the Alps of sex — during May, the last month of the academic year. We were on the daybed after a late start. It was past eleven. Lilly said I had to go home. She was tired and needed to go to bed. I said let me come with you and squeezed both of her nipples in a way I knew she liked. At first she said it was out of the question, and then she said yes, I could come to bed with her and spend the night, but I wouldn't get to put my little man inside her. I could go on caressing her, and I would have to recite poems. This was to help her go to sleep. Getting to bed took a while. Lilly took a shower and made other undisclosed preparations behind the closed door of her bathroom, from which she emerged smelling of soap and toothpaste, her hair moist and carefully brushed, in dark red silk pajamas more splendid than any garment of the sort that I had ever seen. She said I should take a shower as well; she had left a new toothbrush for my use on the side of the washbasin. I did as I was told, but didn't dare to go into the bedroom naked, and it didn't occur to me I could resort to some halfway measure, such as wrapping a towel around my waist. I was still a virgin in the technical sense, and modest. My penis, although handled and licked and even sucked by various girlfriends since the third year of high school, had never yet slid down that channel of which the shape, wet feel and smell I had partially explored with my median finger by the grace of girls not armored by high society undergarments like Lilly's. It doesn't surprise me, therefore, that I settled on a shameful compromise. The memory still galls me. On my knees beside her bed in the darkened bedroom, I had put my hand under the covers and determined that she was still in her pajamas. The reply to my whispered entreaties that she allow me to undress her, was a stern "They stay on." Lacking the courage to go to her entirely naked, and press my denuded, pounding and engorged member against the red silk, I did not take off my boxer shorts.

Later, when I finally did dare to get out of those wretched shorts, it was precisely that contrast between her passivity and being clothed in her luxurious pajamas, and my exigent and blatantly naked desire, that most excited me during the nights with Lilly that followed. I was not to taste pleasure of the same erotic quality until many years later, with a woman who would present herself to me undressed, sitting up on her couch and thrusting her pelvis at me, and insist, especially if I was wearing the scratchy tweed suit that was then my favorite garment, that I penetrate her completely without taking off my trousers, the fly open no more than was functionally indispensable.

To go back to Lilly, though, we both knew that my graduation was not a real leave-taking. She said there would be a letter from her waiting for me at the American Express in Venice. It would tell me the date of her arrival, and where she was to be found. Apart from my having gradually obtained unlimited exploration rights over her body, accorded on condition that I make no attempt to undress her or to push my penis inside her, our lovemaking had not undergone significant change. I continued to recite poetry – a duty that quickly made it necessary to renew my repertory by memorizing poems in the Widener Library where I had a cubicle – and to avoid ejaculation during our caresses and when we were finally asleep. Lilly praised my self-control, and I cannot deny that I came to enjoy it as well. All the same, I was determined that in Venice Lilly would reward my good behavior by accepting the sacrifice of my virginity.

The letter was indeed at the American Express. She wrote that she would be in Venice on Wednesday. I was to meet her at noon that day, at Quadri's, in the Piazza San Marco. She did not tell me at what hotel she planned to stay. The one I had picked out with her help for my lodging, based on the remarkably low prices it charged, was a tiny establishment on Campo S. Angelo. My room was four flights up a steep, narrow and very clean staircase. Though very modest, the hotel seemed altogether clean, and free of any sign of bedbugs, against which Lilly had warned me as generally to be feared in Europe, or indeed any insect life other than mosquitoes. Those swarmed in the room during my first night there because I had not thought of closing the window when I turned on the light. The citronella candle I bought the next day helped. As for bedbugs, I had never seen one in America, and I was not to see one until August of that summer, in a portside hotel in Alicante. So far as I was concerned, there was only one problem with my hotel in Venice. After I had checked in, the portly, dignified lady who seemed to be the owner as well as the receptionist and cashier, looked into my eyes and, wagging her right index finger, said *niente donne nelle stanze*. The injunction was repeated, when I surrendered my room key upon going out to dinner, by a badly shaved night porter. I didn't like having the possibility of bringing Lilly to my room foreclosed, but this, I thought, could not be taken as a significant setback. My room possessed only a washbasin and a chamber pot, which I discovered by accident in the night table. The toilet and the cubicle that housed the bathtub were down the hall. I shared them with the other fourth floor guests. I did not think this arrangement could suit Lilly. We would make love at her hotel, which was bound to be on higher level of sophistication and comfort.

Lilly had said that my first visit to the Accademia and the Scuola S. Rocco must be with her. Therefore, after lunching, as she had recommended, on the Rialto bridge on *seppie* with *polenta* sold by a street vendor – a meal that resulted in a lifelong addiction to those two staples of Venetian cooking – I visited the Doge's Palace. The next day was Tuesday. I went to the Basilica di San Marco first thing in the morning, and lost myself among the crowd of tourists and guides, in solitary contemplation of the mosaics. My knowledge of art and art history was limited to what I had learned in the course I had taken in my last year of high school and through occasional visits to the Fogg in Cambridge, and the Fine Art Museum in Boston, but the Bible had been taught to me very thoroughly. With the aid of the crib sheet I picked up at the postcard stand outside the Basilica, and sometimes on my own, I was able to identify in the stiff gold, green and azure scenes familiar personages and events. As I made my way to the *pala d'oro,* my neck sore from craning it to stare at the ceiling, arches and friezes, I knew that I was changing in ways that might be important.

It was difficult, I found, to go from the huge portraiture of the mosaics to the enamel miniatures that are like oases of calm among the profusion of fiery stones illuminating the *pala.* I stood before it, rubbing my eyes and trying to refocus them without success, and began to think that I would have to postpone looking at the *pala* until another visit, in which it would be the first stop, when I felt a hand descend lightly upon my shoulder. A voice that seemed familiar, although I couldn't immediately place it, pronounced my name. I turned around. The hand and the voice belonged to Hooker Winslow. Tall, imperially thin, with curly blond hair cropped very short, turned out in a suit of pale beige gabardine of the sort I was accustomed to admire on certain of my more elegant fellow-students, Hooker was two years behind me at college. We had lived in the same house on the Charles, and during the academic year that just ended we had taken together a year-long renaissance history seminar. He was very bright, and I was not impervious either to his charm or to the prestige of the family. His father had been twice the governor of Connecticut. Currently, he was its senior U.S. senator. It was common knowledge that the Winslows had been seriously rich since early in the second half of the eighteenth century, with time had multiplied their wealth, and continued to live the way that only the richest Americans had lived before the Great Depression.

It's gorgeous, don't you think? said Hooker and, without waiting for me to answer, added, I had no idea that you would be in Venice. You should have told me. I would have gotten mother to offer you a room. She may not be able to do it now because she has half of father's Senate staff spending their vacation here. By the way, congratulations on all your prizes and honors. I hear you will be spending two years in Paris. That's a brilliant idea. More original than one of the English universities. I am thinking of something along that line myself. Oh, by the way, did you know that I got the same grade from Bellmore on my final paper as you?

Bellmore was the aloof professor who taught the renaissance seminar. He turned up as one of the three readers of my thesis, and, to my surprise, as a member of the panel before which I passed the oral examination that determined my academic honors. Once again I had to try to refocus, this time on the breathless mixture of questions and information that was characteristic of Hooker's speech. I answered as best I could, keeping to the order of his salvos, explaining that I had not had until that moment reason to think that he would be in Venice or that his family might be willing to lodge me, that I wouldn't have imagined imposing my presence on his parents, and that I wasn't in the least surprised that he had done well with Bellmore. Then I doubled back, and admitted that I was confused by the *pala*. I had been staring at it hard, but was somehow unable to make sense of what I saw.

This is your first time, isn't it, said Hooker. In that case, your response is very natural. It's a work that requires getting used to – like a cubist Picasso! You mustn't be afraid to look at it detail by detail, instead of trying to take it all in. Think of it as the Basilica in microcosm! Would you let me lead you through the *pala*?

Without waiting for an answer, Hooker told me of his family's long involvement with the conservation and restoration of San Marco and its various treasures, and how it had resumed directly after the War with the *pala* being its particular object, so that he knew it as though he had lived with it as a neighbor. That explanation finished, he plunged into the history of this extraordinary object, and the meaning of each scene. I found that once I began to follow his advice and looked at the parts, instead of trying to grasp the whole, I could recognize the incidents in the life of Christ, and the career of the Virgin. The scenes taken from the lives of the Apostles called for specific knowledge I didn't have. Hooker possessed it in abundance. To say that he told me the content of the miniatures does not do justice to his exposition: he showed how the unearthly beauty and pathos of the miniatures could be savored as singular phenomena, even if one was ignorant of the events the nameless craftsmen had intended to portray. This was a way of looking at art that ran contrary to the overwhelming need I felt at the time to master the historical background of everything with which I came into contact. I told Hooker sincerely that I admired his knowledge and ability to communicate it, and that I was grateful. He waved away the compliment, and said it was lucky he could talk about art since he was planning to devote himself to studying and teaching it, a decision that his parents were encouraging.

We left the *pala* and walked back toward the baptistery. Stopping here and there, Hooker seemed to be giving me a flash quiz on the mosaics. I enjoyed his conversation and enthusiasm, and was relieved to see that my answers seemed satisfactory. In fact, I was wondering whether I could propose that we meet again, and if I did, how to avoid both being too forward and interfering with what Lilly might want to do, when Hooker took that matter out of my hands. Look, he said, I can't ask you to lunch at home today. Mother is entertaining our ambassador to Italy, and I think there is no room at the table. It's all assigned seats, ceremony, and so on. But what about tomorrow or the next day? I'll tell father about your fellowship. He will want to meet you.

Tomorrow was when I expected Lilly. I explained to Hooker who she was, I hope without hinting at my attachment to her, and about our date at Quadri's that day, and was going to suggest something in the days that followed. He interrupted, and said that to agree on lunch on the day she arrived without consulting her was perhaps a bit brusque, but we should do it the day after, with her if I liked. He would count on her and meet us at Quadri's even though, all things weighed, he preferred Florian's. That was the family café. If there was a problem, I was to telephone him. His mother was very relaxed about such matters if there was advance notice.

I sensed that something was not quite right between Lilly and me – in any event that her conception of our meeting in Venice didn't correspond to the tryst I had imagined and about which we had murmured on her daybed – almost as soon we sat down at Quadri's. I thought she seemed at most moderately enthusiastic about seeing me, having offered me her cheek to kiss and reproved my attempt to hold her hand while we drank our iced coffees. Moreover, she looked at her watch more than once, which I knew she considered very impolite. She told me she was exhausted from the train ride. We should have lunch, after which she would make some phone calls and take a nap. Depending on the outcome of one phone call, we might have dinner together. If I had no other plans. I did not reply. Instead, I asked about our visit to the Accademia. Let me get organized first, she told me. I haven't had a good night's sleep since I don't know when, I need to go to the hairdresser, and I must write some letters. From that point on, quite bewildered, I left the conversation to her at the café and then over the meal at Harry's Bar, which she had warned me was too impossibly expensive for me. But I was not to worry, she would pay, because she wanted me to have a chance to be able to say I had been there at least once. From lunch we walked directly to her *pensione*, on the Zattere, the one in which Ruskin had once made a prolonged stay. It was my first view of the Accademia Bridge and the Accademia itself, the repository of so many works I longed to see, and of the shade and tranquility of the canals and *calle* of the Dorsoduro. We were at the door of the *pensione* when I asked whether she was going to let me come upstairs and take that nap with her. I have missed you so very much, I told her. She laughed in what seemed to me mock horror, and said it was impossible even to think of my coming to her room. Not in this more than respectable establishment, with a clientele of maiden ladies from Boston and New York and their widowed mothers.

So that was what she intended. My cheeks were burning. I told her I had not thought that in

Venice we would have less freedom than we had in Cambridge, and see so little of each other. Give me the telephone number of the place where you are staying, she replied. Unless I call between seven and seven-thirty, we'll have dinner and talk about you.

I spent what was left of the afternoon at the Accademia, first rushing through it so as not to miss anything. Humbled by all that I had seen, I sat afterward for almost an hour before Titian's Pietà, transfixed by its grandeur. Then, at the hotel, I waited for her to telephone. The call didn't come. We had dinner in a restaurant beyond Campo S. Polo that overlooked an odd little bridge called Ponte Storto. She was gentle with me but quite determined, I thought, to drive home the point that I was too intelligent not to have understood that she didn't intend to sleep with me, in Cambridge, or Venice, or anywhere else. Not that having sexual intercourse was such an important transaction; she had had it with many men she liked less. But she didn't think that whatever we had between us, although very nice, should go further, or get us more involved. I would have other thoughts and occupations in Paris. She wanted to get married to the Italian, if that was possible, and if it wasn't she wanted to be free for an affair that made sense. With me, she might be encumbered by a relationship that led straight into a *cul de sac* but was filled with strong feelings. She advised me to accept her friendship on the terms she offered.

There wasn't much of an answer I could make. The night was dark and the streets through which we walked back to the Zattere so empty that we might as well have been the only living souls left in the city. The windows in which there was a light were but few, the only noise was that of our steps and the slapping of the water. Lilly had taken my arm and I gave way to a daydream that began while we were still at table. In it she began to cling to me as soon as we kissed. A moment later, we sat down on the wall of a canal at the entrance of a *sottoportego.* She offered no resistance when I unbuttoned her blouse and opened her bra and then reached under her skirt and pulled down that terrible undergarment. She thrust her pelvis toward my hand. After a while she told me it was her turn, I was to keep still. Very quickly, she had me in her mouth. I whispered she had to stop, I wouldn't be able to hold out. Come, you little fool, she whispered back, don't you understand that I want you to? She took me again, and started rocking back and forth with her whole body until we were both exhausted. Of course, that is not what happened. She allowed me to kiss her more than once during our walk, and opened her mouth to me, but she didn't let me touch her breasts, and there was no sitting down on a canal wall or leaning against a sleek, cold and humid wall. I asked her about her plans for the next day. She said that in the afternoon she would drive out to visit friends who had a villa on the Brenta. She planned to return on Friday, probably in time for lunch. After lunch, if she did get back, we could go to museums. The visit to the hairdresser on Thursday morning was indispensable.

I did not mention the invitation to lunch at the Winslows, mostly because I feared she would accept it and drive out to the villa a few hours later if necessary. As I had already decided that I would leave Venice as soon as the lunch was over, I preferred not to part from her in front of strangers. I also thought her presence at the Winslows would paralyze me. Sheepishly I told her I was leaving on Friday morning. She said she was sorry, but thought that I was making a wise and courageous decision. We would meet soon in Paris, after I had settled down. Would I let her know my address? I said I would, but at the moment I was not entirely sure that I intended to keep my promise. I do not think that I felt angry or insulted. But I was sad,

108

and wished it could have been otherwise – without quite knowing what "otherwise" meant other than sexual intercourse, as she, with her Bostonian bluestocking's precision, might have chosen to put it.

I met Hooker at Quadri's, having called to say that Lilly had another engagement, imagining that we would walk toward Campo S. Stefano. After examining the plan of Venice that showed the location of the palaces on the Grand Canal, I had come to the conclusion that that was how one reached Palazzo Barbaro, which the Winslows had rented. Instead, he led me to a landing at the Piazzetta and pointed to a gondola larger than the others, with two oarsmen, one as usual on the stern deck and the other at the prow.

That one is ours, he said. The custom will go out of style before long, if you want my opinion, but for the time being the parents stick to it. Hop in!

And so I came to have, unexpectedly, for some minutes the sea view of the Republic so eloquently evoked by Thomas Mann. The Winslow's craft moved swiftly. Soon we were at the Dogana, redoing in reverse a part of the trajectory that had brought me from the railroad station. Then the enormous white pile of the Palazzo loomed above us. We penetrated into the court and mounted to the floor directly above, which Hooker told me was the *piano nobile,* where a manservant in black wearing white gloves handed us on a little tray glasses of something cold and bubbly that I learned was *prosecco*. The Senator and the *signora* will be down in a moment, he told Hooker in English. Increasingly nervous, I stared at the huge space we stood in: dark brown, red and gilt, the floor made of porphyry-colored polished stone that shone except where it was covered by rugs with Chinese figures in them, almost unfurnished except for a little table near the windows giving on the glittering Canal. It had been set for four. The prospect of actually having to converse with the Governor, as I knew he preferred to be called, chilled me. I said to myself that I was flying too high.

Hollywood succeeds astonishingly in imitating life – anyway it used to in that distant time – and life had already then taken to mimicking films. The entrance of the gubernatorial couple was ineffably cinematic. Mrs. Winslow, in a white linen dress that showed her to be as preternaturally slender as Hooker, rushed in first, in a torrent of Italian addressed alternatively to the man in black who had served us the wine and to another man in black with white hair and a white tie in addition to his white gloves who, somehow preserving his dignity, had trotted in after her. She stopped abruptly to throw her arms around Hooker, whispered something in his ear, and turned to me. Mr. Carter, she said, or will you permit me to call you Mark? I am so very pleased, we have heard so much about you, the Governor will...

The rest of what she was going to tell me was lost forever because, at that very moment, resounded the boom of her husband's voice, with greetings of his own. He was even taller than Hooker – a vigorous cadaver attired also in white that set off his mauve summer club tie, the same I suddenly realized as Hooker was sporting that day, and a huge silk square the provenance of which I later understood was not his and his son's club at Harvard but a Jermyn Street shirt maker, who was a supplier to father, mother and son. His hand was prodigious: strong although it didn't crush my fingers, pleasantly cool and vast, so that my own fairly large hand disappeared within it. He too had been mysteriously briefed about me. By Hooker? I would not have supposed that Hooker had paid close attention; there was no reason for it; I had thought I had recognized in him the normal friendly incuriosity of a gentleman. By a member of the Governor's staff who, from an aerie up on the top floor of the palace, had made frantic calls to the

University – of which I suddenly remembered the Governor was an overseer – and managed to locate in sweltering Cambridge a dean of students who had looked in the files? To the newspaper in our town in New Hampshire? There was no conversation of the sort I had apprehended at table. Rather, it was a thorough examination of me, conducted by the Governor, with occasional amicable interjections by Mrs. Winslow, on subjects that ranged from the health of my father – the Governor knew he had been recently made the principal of the high school where he had taught for over fifteen years – through the talent of my baby sister for the violin, all the way to the *pièce de résistance*, which occupied the entire time we devoted to our cold sliced veal in tuna and anchovy sauce, namely my plans for study in Paris and ultimate career. I said I hoped to benefit from the presence of the remarkable teachers with whom I would be working and to get enough research done to start writing a piece on how the decline of a great power – France would be my immediate subject – becomes manifest, often quite abruptly, although its causes have been visible for a long time to those who cared to look. Since I intended to be a military historian, military history might be the prism I used. I turned red, as soon as I gave this explanation, because I realized that I had been pompous. Or even worse, fatuous.

That was not, however, how the Governor or Mrs. Winslow seemed to see it. I don't know about Hooker; during the entire meal he seemed to have to struggle to stop himself from giggling. The Governor said the subject was of immense importance and actuality, and asked me to stay in touch with him. In fact, since young people are usually too shy to call or write, he would make it his business to maintain contact. He asked whether I was absolutely committed to teaching. I said that I wasn't sure; I wanted to do research and to write, and I had to earn my living. Teaching had so far seemed to be the most likely solution. Good, he told me. In time I will have some ideas for you. Then the lunch suddenly ended. Hooker walked back with me to the hotel and told me that curtain came down on lunch at two-thirty no matter what. It was a rule to which there were no exceptions. Otherwise, they would have kept me longer. You have made the best possible impression, he told me. Then he added, My father doesn't waste words. You will indeed hear from him.

Hooker turned out to be quite right in his prediction: the Governor's presence and protection were to be determinative at various turns in my career. I felt a great surge of affection for Hooker and told him I was sorry to be leaving and that I hoped that we too would stay in touch. Having said that, and not wanting to have a fib remain between us, I confessed that things had not gone as I had imagined they might between Lilly and me, and that was the reason I made up the lie about her having plans that interfered with coming to lunch.

That was also the reason for my leaving Venice sooner. He smiled and said that my sin was forgiven. Then, suddenly serious, he told me that we would be meeting often; he was almost as difficult to shake off as his father. There too he was right: we remained friends for a long time, until he died.

I took the train to Rome, because it happened to be leaving a little less than an hour after a gondola deposited me at the station. It amused me to extend Lilly's precept about arrivals to departures. In the scorching third class compartment I opened my eyes in disbelief. Sitting opposite me was a girl who had been in the same Latin classes as I at college during our freshman and sophomore years, and then disappeared. Jane Evans, the Latinist with the face of a tawny hawk, and a hawk's green eyes flecked with gold. That afternoon, she wore a pigeon gray cotton jersey sleeveless dress belted at the waist and sandals. Not for the first time, I found her beautiful. She was reading an Italian language newspaper and did not look up while I was settling down. I waited until she turned a page and said her name. She recognized me immediately. She had left Radcliffe, she told me, to transfer to Sarah Lawrence and be closer to New York. This would be her first visit to Rome as well. Afterward, she intended to travel in Europe until it was time to matriculate at the university in Bologna, where she could study with the man she thought was the greatest classicist alive. A Fulbright fellowship and nothing else was financing her, so the travel had to be on the cheap. I told her we could have a contest to see who would spend less. We both laughed at that, the real reason for our jollity being that we had realized, without a word having been said, that we were going to spend the summer together. Jane had a plan of Rome and a guidebook. Lugging her backpack and my duffel bag, we took a bus from the Termini railroad station to San Silvestro and from there we walked to the Pantheon, holding hands. At some point during our trek, I set down my suitcase and put my arms around Jane and her backpack and drowned my sorrows, already evanescent and oddly distant, in a kiss that she seemed to want as much as I. The two *alberghi* we tried first in the vicinity of the Pantheon were full, but right across the street from the mighty structure we found a *pensione* that had a room on the top floor that was available if I took it for a week and paid in advance. Burnt by the experience in Venice, I told Jane to have an *espresso* next door, while I produced my passport and filled out the registration form. When I went to get her at the café, she was pouting. You are an oaf, she told me. You didn't even bother to ask first whether I would share a room with you!

Jane had a brother at the American Embassy in Rome who was going on home leave. He lent her his little Simca convertible. We drove it over the Pyrenees into Spain, and that is how we found ourselves one night in July in a hulking old hotel that overlooked the harbor, making love on a bed with a brass bedstead to the beat of fireworks that an American cruiser on a visit to Alicante was setting off for the amusement of the local population. Or was it also a gentle reminder of our naval power to be communicated to the appropriate government circles in Madrid? The latter thought did not occur to me immediately, although the fireworks made a noise indistinguishable from the soundtrack of naval bombardments in any number of World War II movies I had seen. My mind was fixed on how Jane and I had become one throbbing body, not on military history or politics. For all our ardor, we were gradually distracted from pleasure by bites that were not bites we were giving each other, and the unbearable itching that followed. We stopped. I turned on the light, for the moment indifferent to mosquitoes, and there they were, the little red points that Lilly had warned me against, scurrying in all directions on the sheet. We shook off the sheet, discovered that the blanket, even on close inspection, looked clean, and spent the rest of that night on the stone floor nursed to sleep by love and the salvoes of our Mediterranean fleet.

I have said love. It was love, and it proved strong enough for Jane and me to marry after my time was up in Paris, but not resilient enough to survive the years that followed at Harvard while we wrote our dissertations and obtained our degrees. There were no children. We parted as friends, to the extent that such a thing is ever possible. Jane remained at the university to teach Virgil, Ovid and Lucretius. At the urging of Governor Winslow, I did not take up the university appointment that was offered to me and joined instead, at the beginning of the Kennedy administration, the policy planning group at the State Department. My dissertation had become a book on the vacuum in the political center of Europe that resulted from French military weakness, and the consequent decline of France, which I judged irreversible. It was well received. Within a short period of time I found I had a reputation in the circles that counted for me. Working for the government, however, severely limited my ability to publish, and I was becoming restless. The Governor urged patience. Besides, I agreed that the call to serve that president took priority over personal ambition. The assassination in Dallas, and the aggressive policy in Vietnam that began with the advent of the new administration, changed everything. I had no doubt that the war policy was misconceived and nefarious, and wanted to distance myself from it and its proponents. The Governor didn't think I was wrong. I resigned from the State Department and went to live in Paris. There was an opportunity to teach a course that interested me at the school of political science while I pursued my own work.

So it happened that in 1966 I attended a Thanksgiving lunch in Paris given by the political counselor of our Embassy – in reality the resident representative of the CIA – whom I knew well from Washington, and his wife, a food writer for the *Herald Tribune.* Among the guests I discovered Lilly. She and the food critic had been in the same class at Smith. I had not seen Lilly more than three or four times since we said goodbye in Venice, at a concert in Boston and cocktail parties in Cambridge. But gossip about her abounded, and I was familiar with it. She was working on the personal staff of a very important and powerful political figure. His taste for women of Lilly's age or preferably younger, who resembled pretty and vivacious schoolteachers and were of excellent family, was well known. It was standard for him to keep two or three or four of them on his staff, which some said he really considered his harem, serious political work being done by male consultants. The general view was that Lilly deserved better. She had not changed really, except that she was thinner, which was becoming, and, to use an expression that was habitual with her, she was really pulled together. Her hair and fingernails were testimony to care that was more sophisticated and perhaps more intensive than they had been used to receive from the establishment at the Boston Ritz she had used to frequent. She wore a tweed suit so beautifully cut, and of such subtle color, that even I could recognize in it the hand of a couturier. She was living in New York, she told me, on East 64th Street, when she wasn't in Washington. Her mother had been dead for three years. The professor father had remarried. She had little reason to return to Cambridge.

When I asked what she was doing in Paris, she informed me that the political figure had been here, bringing his personal staff, and therefore her, and now was in Brussels, having Thanksgiving with our ambassador who had been his college classmate. He would be returning in a couple of days, and then she thought the whole group would move on to London. The political figure was to give a speech before the Oxford Union. Would I like to meet him, she inquired. In those politically explosive times, he was a Republican for whose foreign and military policy views, and, I should say, good faith, I had respect. So did Governor Winslow, notwithstanding party differences. I said yes, with pleasure, if that could be conveniently arranged. He will want to see you, she told me, and wrote down my address and telephone number in a little red Hermès pocket diary. Then she wanted to know about my work. I explained as much as I could without taking too great a risk of boring her. She offered me both cheeks to kiss when we said goodbye on the sidewalk.

I lived on the rue de Vaugirard, near the Luxembourg. The mania for codes that you must punch in to open the door of your building had not yet reached mine. After the lunch, I went to a movie on the Champs-Elysées and had a croque monsieur and a glass of red wine afterward. I got home around nine, went upstairs, finding Lilly curled up on the floor before my door. She was asleep or passed out. Perhaps there exists a combination of both. In any case, the smell of hard of liquor was quite strong. I shook her awake. She brightened up almost at once and said, Oh my, you have made me wait. We went into the apartment, which had the uneasy aspect of places where you live quite alone, without a cat or dog, and nothing moves when you are out unless the burglars have stopped by. That had not happened. I installed Lilly in an armchair in the living room, turned lights on everywhere, and showed her the way to the bathroom. She emerged very chirpy, although I had heard the heavy sound of retching. I proposed coffee or tea, which she refused. Whiskey was what she wanted. Reluctantly, I gave her a highball, and produced another, much weaker, for myself. The bastard, she said, the dirty bastard. Little by little it came out. After the food critic's bash, she had gone to a party that the great political figure's staffers were throwing at the apartment of a *New York Times* correspondent who had covered many of their boss's campaigns, and, in the course of it she learned, from a casual remark, that another member of the harem, who manifestly was not present at the party, wasn't there because she had been taken by the great man to Brussels. The lying bastard, she said. He said I couldn't come because the ambassador had been an usher at his wedding to that goose to whom he is still married, and naturally he wouldn't understand. What wouldn't he understand? That his classmate fucks me? Where has that dunderhead lived? Doesn't he read the newspaper? She cried after that. When she stopped, she told me that I had remained her friend, probably the only one, and that she had hoped since the start that it would be so, that nothing between us could change. She spotted my record player and with complete equilibrium – really agility – went over to the shelf where I kept my records, picked out "Dido and Aeneas," and put it on the turntable. It's music I love, and I was glad to listen to it with her. One by one, she played all my Purcell records. She had found my whiskey bottle and ice bucket and bottles of soda, and installed these supplies on the coffee table. Remember my daybed? she asked. Tables are turned now. It's your couch, your whiskey, your records, your apartment, your Paris. I have nothing.

I didn't know how to answer, but I knew I must get her home. My car is in the courtyard, I told her. That too was new, that I should have a car. Please let me drive you to your hotel.

Never, she replied. Never. I will not go back to that bastard or his herd of swine. If you throw me out, I will sleep on the *berges* of the Seine. I will go to Pont Neuf and throw myself into the river.

I saw that she was once again drunk. The bed in my guestroom was made up. I said, All right, I have a nice room and a nice bed for you. You've been

127

through a lot today. You should go to bed. You slept in my bed, she answered. I'm not going to your gue-stroom, I am going to your bed with you. Don't worry. You won't have to put your little man inside me. I know that it's disgusting to fuck a drunk.

Of course, we went to bed together, she undressed and I in my pajamas, and there was no keeping my penis out of her because that wasn't what she had in mind. It was not like anything I had expected, our long-postponed sexual intercourse. Somehow I had imagined that with the life she had led, about some of which she had told me, and the political figure's presumed need of spicy dishes, she would be very inventive, but it was instead like making love to a girl you had always known and had been married to for many years.

It wasn't what you thought it would be? she asked the next morning at breakfast.

I shook my head and said it wasn't, but perhaps because of that I had liked it all the more.

I thought you would, she said. Then she added, it seemed to me à propos of nothing: I was in Beaune last weekend, at the dinner of the Tastevins. He – here she named the great political figure – was made a grand officer or commander in chief or God knows what. Everybody had a huge hangover on Sunday morning, but I went to the cathedral and cried and prayed for all of us. I prayed for you.

She left almost immediately afterward.

I didn't know what she meant by "all of us." Perhaps it was nothing more than all her family and friends. Perhaps some grand allusion was rattling about in her mind, hangovers being often father to odd associations of ideas, something on the order of Gertrude Stein's "you are all a lost generation." It didn't matter. She had moved me deeply by what she said, and the feeling continued to germinate until I saw her next. By that time, the great political figure was no more, having died suddenly, leaving in disarray his harem, his political machine and much more. Lilly, I knew, had moved briefly back to Cambridge, and then – astonishingly – married a man a good fifteen years older than she, who had made a pile of money in real estate in Hawaii, called it quits, and decided to devote himself to his true passion, politics of the extreme right. To that end, he bought a string of small and medium size newspapers in the Southwest that were preaching his gospel. Lilly and he lived in Tucson. Given Lilly's background and convictions, not to speak of her service to the liberal Republican tradition through all she had done for the great political figure, her taking that man and staying with him was inconceivable. Yet it was perfectly true. It made for a great deal of tongue-clucking among those of us who remembered the old days in Cambridge, the Poets' Theater, and knew Lilly's more recent history.

I was living in New York again, and one evening, soon after the first inauguration of Ronald Reagan, was having dinner with Hooker at Giovanni's.

Hooker had been married and divorced twice; I had not remarried. At the end of the previous academic year, he had been elevated to the rank of university professor at Harvard, the youngest person ever to have received that honor. I had just published the book I had been dreaming of since high school, which traced the consequences of Sadowa through the victory of the allied powers in World War I. We were lost in our talk and antipasti when, in that way one has knowing that someone is staring at one without having actually turned one's head, became aware of a presence on the other side of the room. I did look, and there was Lilly with a man who corresponded to my idea of what her husband would be like. Before I could make a move to greet them, they both came over to our table. Hooker and I rose. Introductions were made. The husband began to talk about my book, and about how we must get to know each other during the many visits they made to New York and the pied à terre they maintained at the Sherry Netherland. I said that would be lovely, when I returned from Europe. I was leaving for an extended vacation that would start in Venice.

Venice, said Lilly. I taught you the most important rule about it, how you must arrive in a gondola. Do you remember?

Every word you uttered, I replied. As though you had spoken only yesterday. They went back to their table, and Hooker, whose memory never failed him, put his hand on my forearm, and, squeezing it affectionately, said: Why that is the girl you met in Venice! I nodded. After a moment of silence, we resumed our conversation.

Venice:
Reflections of a Novelist

by Louis Begley

Venice: It is a great pleasure to write the word, but I am not sure there is not a certain impudence in pretending to add anything to it. Venice has been painted and described many thousands of times, and of all the cities of the world it is the easiest to visit without going there. Open the first book and you will find a rhapsody about it; step into the first picture dealer's and you will find three or four high-coloured "views" of it. There is notoriously nothing more to be said on the subject.

The voice is not mine; it is Henry James's, who famously and fortunately disregarded his own advice by writing again and again about *la serenissima.* As a novelist, I have obviously disregarded his counsel as well, and I am about to disregard it again now. The charming essay from which I have just quoted may be found in the collection of James's travel pieces known as *Italian Hours.* Two instances of James's transgressions as a writer of fiction, of his use of Venice as a setting for all or a part of his story, are *The Aspern Papers,* which ran in *The Atlantic* from March to May 1888, and *The Wings of the Dove,* published in 1902, when James had just passed the age of fifty-nine. I find it extraordinarily moving, and mention it out of reverence, and an ever-increasing sense of wonder, that the next two years saw the publication of two more of his master-pieces, each equal in scope to *The Wings,* and each as clearly a work of genius: *The Ambassadors,* in 1903, and *The Golden Bowl,* in 1904. With those three works finished, his life's work as a novelist, although not as a man of letters, was over. Twelve years later, on February 28, 1916, James died.

I have been visiting Venice since 1954. In the 1980s, visits to Venice became an unquestioned annual event, one that my wife and I have come to regard as a fixed part of our lives. The rush of pleasure is just as intense when we first see from the water taxi we boarded at the airport the outline of the city glimmering in the morning haze; we still find that the way we live in Venice goes well with our work; our painter son who has lived in Rome for many years, and whose knowledge of Venetian *calli* and *rii* and *sottoporteghi*, and of the contents of the sacristies of out-of-the-way churches, is almost as surprising as my wife's, has continued to spend harmonious days with us, organized around lunches and dinners, which we eat late to safeguard the working hours during which we are not to be disturbed. I had the great good luck to get to know the work of Marcel Proust and Thomas Mann long before I first went to Venice: Mann's beginning in 1949, when I read *Death in Venice*, "Mario the Magician," and "Disorder and Early Sorrow," and Proust's in the spring of 1951, when during one semester I made my way through all of *À la recherche du temps perdu.* It was also in the early 1950s, although I cannot pinpoint the year, that I began to read Henry James, at first probably some of the stories and perhaps *The Turn of the Screw* and *Washington Square,* and later, but while I was still at college, the longer works. Certainly, I had read *The Wings of the Dove* by the summer of 1954. I have a life-long unshakable habit of peering at people, events and places through works of fiction I admire, as though they were so many different pairs of glasses, each of which in its own way adjusts my vision. Accordingly, I have no reason to doubt my memory of having looked at Venice from the start as Venice of James and Proust and Mann.

We change over the years, and so does the way we read. We come to know more about life and the art of fiction as well. In 1989, I wrote my first novel, and realized that my understanding of how another author's work was actually composed had become more acute. As my visits to Venice became frequent and I got to know the city better, questions occurred to me about the works of fiction associated with it that I admire the most. I wanted to know how these three great men – James, Proust and Mann – had "worked it." I am using consciously a Jamesian expression because it seems so suited to what a writer must do. Each of them had used Venice as a setting for an important part of his plot. Was there a particular reason for that choice? Was Venice used only as a splendid stage set, or was there a more necessary, organic connection; had the choice Venice work added something beyond pages of dazzling descriptions? In the background was my awareness, based on a growing accumulation of experience, of how a novelist, having invented his characters, the predicament in which they find themselves, and having settled on the narrative technique and the tone of voice he will use, must then undertake the unforgiving and hidden task of actually keeping the story moving from incident to incident. He must situate the action somewhere, and he is not always free to choose one location over another. A particular setting may be necessary, because otherwise the story will not make sense or may lack verisimilitude. At other times, there is no such constraint, and the author is free to follow his whim. Of course, the limitations imposed by one's knowledge are always present, and those who disregard them do so at their great peril. I asked myself how the success of choices that are not forced by the requirements of the plot should be measured. By the power of descriptive passages alone, or should one look for more? Is it not fair to expect that the setting will be an organic part of the story, enhancing its dramatic interest? As I considered these questions, I read once again the irresistible novels that had inspired them.

The source of *The Aspern Papers* was an anecdote told to James in Florence, in 1887, about a certain Captain Silsbee, an American art critic and "Shelley-worshipper," who learns that Miss Claremont, an aged former mistress of Lord Byron, the mother of his daughter Allegra, and half-sister of Shelley's second wife, is living in Florence with a middle-aged niece, and has in her possession correspondence between Shelley and Byron that has been kept completely secret. Silsbee determines to get hold of the letters at any cost, and inveigles himself into the two ladies' residence as a lodger. The Misses Claremont are very poor. He hopes that if the older lady dies while he is still effectively a member of the household the niece will sell the letters to him. The scheme comes close to fruition. However, it turns out that the niece does not want money. She tells Silsbee: "I will give you all the letters if you marry me!" – whereupon Silsbee finds the cost too high and flees, and, as James put it in his notebooks, *"court encore."* "Delicacy had demanded, I felt," James wrote in the Preface to the 1910 New York edition of *The Aspern Papers*,

> that my appropriation of the Florentine legend should purge it, first of all of references too obvious; so that, to begin with, I shifted the scene of the adventure. Juliana [the elder Miss Bordereau substituted, in *The Aspern Papers,* for the aunt] was thinkable only in Byronic and more or less immediately post-Byronic Italy; but there were conditions in which she was ideally arrangeable, as it happened, especially in respect to the later time and the long undetected survival; there

being absolutely no refinement of the mouldy rococo, in human or whatever other form that you may not disembark at the dislocated water steps of almost any decayed monument of Venetian greatness in auspicious quest of... It was a question, in fine, of covering one's tracks; and I felt that I couldn't cover mine more than in postulating a comparative American Byron to match an American Miss Clairmont – she as absolute as she would. I scarce know whether best to say for this device today that it cost me little or that it cost me much; it was "cheap" or expensive according to the degree of verisimilitude artfully obtained.

The American Byron whom James postulated and invented as the celebrated poet once in love with Miss Juliana Bordereau is Jeffrey Aspern; he substituted for the English Misses Clairmont the aged Miss Juliana Bordereau and her grand-niece Tina "of minor antiquity," Americans of a type not unfamiliar in Europe of the nineteenth century, "shy, mysterious and, as was somehow supposed, scarcely respectable...believed to have lost in their long exile all national quality." James lodged them in a palazzo that

> was not particularly old, only two or three
> centuries; and it had an air not so much
> of decay as of quiet discouragement, as
> if it had rather missed its career.

Of course, Juliana and Tina "live on nothing, for they have nothing to live on." Out of Silsbee, James fashioned the narrator, an American historian and publisher living in England, a man so obsessed with the poet's literary remains that, as he tells his friend and patroness in Venice, Mrs. Prest, "there's no baseness I wouldn't commit for Jeffrey Aspern's sake." From the experience of his English publishing partner, who was rebuffed by Miss Juliana in his quest for the correspondence, the narrator knows that the old lady will not admit to possessing it, and certainly will not part with it. Mrs. Prest inspires him with a Silsbee-like device: "Simply make them take you in on the footing of a lodger." That is what he does, and lays siege to Miss Tina, hoping that somehow through her he will be able to make sure that the correspondence is there and remains in safety, and that, if he manages to be present when the old lady dies, he will have a leg up in dealing over it with the executors or Miss Tina herself. Fate treats him as it treated Silsbee: too kindly. Juliana does die while he is still a lodger in the palazzo but, like the younger Miss Clairmont, Miss Tina makes clear that he can have the papers only if he becomes her husband. And like Silsbee the narrator flees. Unlike Silsbee, he returns – to find that Miss Tina, in her beautiful delicacy, understood the unspoken rejection, and took the only action consistent with her honor, one that would put an end to her and the narrator's temptations. She has burned the Aspern papers, sheet by sheet.

Perhaps because he moved the action of *The Aspern Papers* to Venice and away from Florence out of his own sense of delicacy, and not for a reason inherent in the story, I find that James used "the city of exhibition," as he called it, principally as a backdrop, and added personages and activities that may be said to be "typically Venetian" merely to fill the stage and enliven the plot, and to create the necessary atmosphere. Thus he gives us Mrs. Prest, made in the image of the rich, bossy, competent and meddlesome American women living in Europe who appear regularly in James's work. He makes use of the gondola – that symbol of Venetian life that has overtaken the lion of St. Mark in recognition by readers and in richness of instant connotations. Thus the narrator has a gondolier attached to him, one Pasquale, who can manage and arrange anything he is asked to do. The instant availability of a gondola hugely impresses Miss Tina, who hasn't been in one for many years. (It is amusing to note that a gondolier named Pasquale makes a brief appearance in *The Wings of the Dove,* as well.) James also provides a thumbnail sketch of the two maiden ladies' life and the society in which they move:

> They had seen all the curiosities; they had even been to the Lido in a boat...they had a collation there, brought in three baskets and spread on the grass. I [the narrator] asked her what kind of people they had known and she said, Oh very nice ones – the Cavaliere Bombicci and the Contessa Altemura, with whom they

had had a great friendship! Also English people – the Churtons and the Goldies and Mrs Stock-Stock, whom they loved dearly; she was dead and gone, poor dear. That was the case with most of their kind circle – this expression was Miss Tina's own; though a few were left, which was a wonder considering how they had neglected them. She mentioned the names of two or three Venetian old women; of a certain doctor, very clever, who was so attentive – he came as a friend, he had really given up practice; of the *avvocato* Pochintesta, who wrote beautiful poems and had addressed one to her aunt. These people came to see them without fail every year, usually at the *capo d'anno*...if the good Venetians liked you once they liked you forever.

Clearly, James did not go to very much trouble over this; the names he gives these walk-on spear-carriers are intentionally comical, as though to make sure that the reader does not fail to realize that the Master is amusing himself. Had Miss Juliana and Miss Tina traveled to the Prato in a carriage, instead of being conveyed to the Lido in a boat, and the word Florentine been used instead of Venetian, we would be in Florence.

It's a different matter when it comes to the evocation of the sights and the feeling of Venice. This is done with his great economy of means, more through suggestion than any specificity of description, but the city comes wonderfully alive. (James's minimalist technique may be seen at its highest perfection in *The Ambassadors,* where he creates Paris with just a sentence here and there making entire neighborhoods rise up before the reader's eyes.) The palazzo that Miss Juliana and Miss Tina reside in has attached to it a large garden.

Such palaces on out of the way canals haven't changed and there are very many of them. Nevertheless, three bridges away from the Scuola di San Giorgio degli Schiavoni stands one of them that seemed to me so like Miss Juliana's that for a long time I was convinced I had identified the two ladies' palace, the mood about it seemed so right. I had no other indications to guide me. Now I am inclined to think that they lived instead at Palazzo Cappello Layard, in Dorsoduro. Here is what James did with the palace garden; the narrator is speaking:

> I had an arbour arranged and a low table and an armchair put into it; and I carried out books and portfolios – I had always some business of writing in hand – and worked and waited and mused and hoped, while the golden hours elapsed and the plants drank in the light and the inscrutable old palace turned pale and

then, as the day waned, began to recover and flush and my papers rustled in the wandering breeze of the Adriatic.

And here is a description of the Piazza San Marco:

I sat in front of Florian's café eating ices, listening to music, talking with acquaintances: the traveller will remember how the immense cluster of tables and little chairs stretches like a promontory into the smooth lake of the Piazza. The whole place, of a summer's evening, under the stars and with all the lamps, all the voices and light footsteps on the marble – the only sounds of the immense arcade that encloses it – is an open-air saloon dedicated to cooling drinks and to a still finer degustation, that of the splendid impressions received during the day...

The great basilica, with its low domes and bristling embroideries, the mystery of its mosaic and sculpture, looked ghostly in the tempered gloom, and the sea-breeze passed between the twin columns of the Piazzetta, the lintels of a door no longer guarded, as gently as if a rich curtain swayed there.

It is interesting to compare this description of eating ices at Florian's and seeing the Piazza in its summertime mood of mellow evening melancholy with the Piazza's very different aspect in the description I quote below, from *The Wings of the Dove.*

In contrast to the rather perfunctory use made of it in *The Aspern Papers,* Venice of *The Wings of the Dove,* is powerfully one of James's important *dramatis personae.* He draws, of course, on his intimate knowledge of Venice as tourist, travel writer, and art critic, his stays with Mrs. Arthur Bronson at her Casa Alvisi, almost directly across the Grand Canal from the Salute, and, more directly relevant to *The Wings,* the extended visits to Daniel and Ariana Curtis, who owned Palazzo Barbaro, on the same side of the Canal as Casa Alvisi, but nearer the Accademia Bridge. Palazzo Barbaro is generally thought to have been the model for Palazzo Leporelli, which Milly Theale rents. Mrs. Bronson and Mrs. Curtis were great international hostesses of the day. Through their salons passed American expatriates meandering in and out of Venice — the motley crowd of the wellborn and the not so wellborn, seeking in Europe culture and the low cost of living that made princely (or at least high bourgeois) dwellings and uncounted servants affordable to remittance men. Their milieu held no secrets for James. Finally, by the time James wrote *The Wings,* a link of personal tragedy had been established between him and Venice. In January 1894, his beloved friend, Constance Fenimore Woolson, in whose villa in Florence he was staying when he wrote *The Aspern Papers*, fell – or more likely leaped – to her death from an upper story of her Venetian palazzo.

Oversimplified brutally, the action of *The Wings* is centered an unequal struggle between two of James's most splendid female creations over one of his more insipid male characters, Merton Densher, a creature of the sort redeemed in England of the nineteenth century by being generally considered a gentleman. Today, we would say he was a wimp. Kate Croy, triumphantly beautiful, determined and penniless, makes me think of the "Victory of Samothrace" that greets the visitor at the top of the great staircase in the Louvre. Her friend and victim, Milly Theale, the dove of *The Wings* is "the last fine flower – blooming alone, for the fullest attestation of her freedom – of an 'old' New York stem." James thought that young

Americans like her were heirs to all the ages: her true inheritance was to live her life to the full. James made Milly sublime, both physically and spiritually. But orphaned, bereft of "almost every human appendage," colossally rich, she is also "stricken." Stricken by what? The nature of the ailment is never mentioned, much less explained, and yet it is of exceeding gravity, and all understand that she may die of it at any moment. However, as we get to know Milly better, and are at her side when she consults in London the great medical man, Sir Luke Strett, we are led to guess that the malady may be as much moral as physical. It can be held at bay, provided that Milly's will to live holds. He tells her

> You've the right to be happy. You must accept any form in which happiness may come.

"Oh, I'll accept any whatever!" Milly replies "almost gaily." And at the end of the interview, when she asks the great man whether she will live, his answer is: "My dear young lady…isn't to 'live' exactly what I'm trying to persuade you to take the trouble to do?" He agrees with her project of settling for some months in Venice; his ears perk up when he hears that she and her companion, Mrs. Stringham, and Kate Croy and Kate's aunt Mrs. Lowder, will not be only ladies together. Merton Densher will be there are well.

Both Sir Luke and Milly understand that, in order to live, Milly needs to love. She is, in fact, in love with Merton Densher, whose attractiveness to women I cannot fathom. Alas, it isn't enough for Milly to love: she needs also to be loved, and in this case that cannot be. Densher has no money but he loves Kate Croy, and Kate loves him. Their attachment is secret, and must remain such because Kate's indispensable rich aunt, Mrs. Lowder, has another idea for Kate: she wants her to marry Lord Mark. Kate concocts a devilish scheme: She tells Milly that she, Kate, does not care for Densher. That allows Milly to love him with a clear conscience; Densher in turn has been ordered by Kate to allow Milly to believe that he does love her — she is so regal that she may propose marriage to him, relieving him of the need to take a first step that is surely beyond his power; if the scheme works, Densher and Milly will marry; and, before too long, Milly will die, making Densher rich. Rich enough for him and Kate to marry, and to live happily ever after in a manner appropriate to Kate's natural high style. Lord Mark derails the scheme. He too needs money, and has a plan not unlike Kate's: he thinks he can get money from a brief marriage to Milly. Not a bit shy, he comes to Venice and proposes. Milly loses no time turning him down. Lord Mark understands at once that Densher is his fortunate rival, and is able to worm out of Milly that her hope of being loved by Densher is based on Kate's lie about the relations between her and the young man. Some weeks later, Lord Mark takes his revenge. He calls on Milly again, and tells her that Kate and Densher are secretly engaged. The news is a fatal blow. Soon, Densher learns that Milly has "turned her face to the wall."

Here is how James makes Venice an active participant in this masque of love and betrayal. First, Palazzo Leporelli, is the "ark" in Milly Theale's "deluge." Her *corriere,* assisting her in her travels on the continent, is "the great Eugenio, recommended by grand-dukes and Americans." We have moved to a sphere far higher than that of Pasquale, the gondolier in *The Aspern Papers.* If we are Jamesians, we know this corriere, having seen his more vulgar incarnations, notably in *Daisy Miller.* Eugenio finds the palazzo, having taken in Millie's explanation that in Venice she wants, please, if possible, no dreadful, no vulgar hotel; but, if it can at all be managed — you know what I mean — some fine old rooms, wholly independent, for a series of months. Plenty of them, too, and the more interesting the better: part of a palace, historic and picturesque, but strictly inodorous, where we shall be to ourselves, with a cook, don't you know? — with servants, frescoes, tapestries, antiquities, the thorough make believe of a settlement.

She gets her wish:

Not yet so much as this morning had she felt herself sink into possession: gratefully glad that the warmth of the southern summer was still in the high, florid rooms, palatial chambers where hard, cool pavements took reflections in their lifelong polish, and where the sun on the stirred sea-water, flickering up through open windows, played over the painted "subjects" in the splendid ceilings – medallions of purple and brown, of brave old melancholy colour, medals as of old reddened gold, embossed and beribboned, all toned with time and flourished and scolloped and gilded about, set in their great moulded and figured concavity (a nest of white cherubs, friendly creatures of the air), and appreciated by the aid of that second tier of smaller lights, straight openings to the front, which did everything, even with the Baedekers and photographs of Milly's party dreadfully meeting the eye, to make the place an apartment of state.

Densher will see the palace in a very different light, after Lord Mark has denounced him to Milly, and she has told the servants that she is no longer at home for him. The poor man, accustomed to dine at the palazzo every evening, he who "had not been at Palazzo Leporelli, among the receivable, but had taken his place once and for all among the involved and included," arrives in a driving autumnal storm to call on Milly and her companion, Mrs. Stringham at teatime, only to learn that:

> Neither of the two ladies it appeared received, and yet Pasquale [the combination manservant and gondolier] was not prepared to say that either was not well. He was not yet prepared to say that either *was* well, and he would have been blank, Densher mentally observed, if the term could ever apply to members of a race in whom vacancy was but a nest of

darknesses — not a vain surface, but a place of withdrawal in which something obscure, something always ominous, indistinguishably lived.

Thus rebuffed, Densher asks to see the great Eugenio, who has hitherto been friendly to him, and

with whom for three rich minutes protected from the weather he was confronted in the gallery that led from the watersteps to the court...

The weather from early morning, had turned to storm, the first sea-storm of the autumn, and Densher had almost invidiously brought [Eugenio] down the outer staircase — the massive ascent, the great feature of the court, to Milly's *piano nobile.* This was to pay him — it was the one chance — for the vulgar view that, clever and not rich, the young man from London was – by the obvious way – after Miss Theale's fortune.

Eugenio stands firm, Densher doesn't break through, and

This manner, while they stood for a long minute facing each other over all they didn't say, played a part as well in the sudden jar to Densher's protected state. It was a Venice all of evil that had broken out for them alike, so that they were together in their anxiety, if they really could have met on it; a Venice of cold lashing rain from a low black sky, of wicked wind raging through narrow passes, of general arrest and interruption, with the people engaged in all the waterlife huddled, stranded and wageless, bored and cynical, under archways and bridges...

Now Densher leaves the palazzo:

> He had to walk in spite of the weather, and he took his course, through crooked ways, to the Piazza where he should have the shelter of the galleries. Here, in the high arcade, half of Venice was crowded close, while, on the Molo, at the limit of the expanse, the old columns of St. Mark and of the Lion were like the lintels of a door wide open to the storm...The wet and the cold were now to reckon with, and it was precisely to Densher, as if he had seen the obliteration, at a stroke, of the margin on a faith in which they were all living. The margin had been his

name for it – the thing that though it had held out, could bear no shock. The shock, in some form had come, and he wondered about it while, threading his way among loungers as vague as himself, he dropped his eyes sightlessly on the rubbish in shops. There were stretches of the gallery paved with squares of red marble, greasy now with the salt spray; and the whole place, in its huge elegance, the grace of its conception and the beauty of its detail, was more than ever like a great drawing-room, the drawing-room of Europe, profaned and bewildered by some reverse of fortune.

Just about at that moment, Densher suddenly sees through the window of Florian's, inside the café, the face of an acquaintance seated, well within range, at a small table on which a tumbler, half emptied and evidently neglected, still remained, and though he had on his knee, as he leaned back, a copy of a French newspaper – the heading of the *Figaro* was visible – he stared straight before him at the little opposite rococo wall.

It's Lord Mark. Immediately, Densher understands what has happened. "It was a great thing," James tells us, "for Densher to get this answer."

He held it close, he hugged it, quite leaned on it as he continued to circulate…it explained – and that was much, for with explanations he might somehow deal. The vice in the air, otherwise, was too much like the breath of fate. The weather had changed, the rain was ugly, the wind wicked, the sea impossible, *because* of Lord Mark.

Slowly, the reader is brought to realize that Venice is an integral part of the novel's *dénouement* and success. Specifically, Palazzo Leporelli – that splendid jewel box covered by a patina of rich history and lapped by water – makes possible momentary compliance with Sir Luke Strett's injunction that Milly accept happiness in any form, and her obtaining "the sense of having lived". We see this nowhere better than in the following passage, which immediately precedes Lord Mark's first visit:

> She made now, alone, the full circuit of the place, noble and peaceful while the summer sea, stirring here and there a curtain or an outer blind, breathed into its veiled places. She had a vision of clinging to it; that perhaps Eugenio

could manage. She was *in* it, as in the ark of her deluge, and filled with such tenderness for it that why shouldn't this, in common mercy be warrant enough? She would never, never leave it – she would engage to that; she would ask nothing more than to sit tight in it and float on and on.

Milly's palace is simply inconceivable in any place other than Venice. The quality of Venice as a small town, in which tourists cross and re-cross daily the Piazza and congregate in it, so that, short of being masked, one is fatally seen and found out, favors Lord Mark's treachery – because he is able to connect immediately Densher's presence in the city with Milly's rejection of himself – and makes totally convincing the recognition scene at Florian's. As soon as Densher sees Lord Mark, he too knows why the other man is there, there being only a very limited number of reasons to account for his being there, as well as the nature of the consequent catastrophe.

Proust did not have nearly the same deep personal experience of Venice as James. In all, he was there twice. The first visit, which he made with his mother over a period of three weeks in May 1900 – thus two years before the publication of *The Wings of the Dove* – was largely a pilgrimage devoted to the work of John Ruskin. Part One of Proust's important article on Ruskin had appeared in the *Gazette des Beaux Arts*; he was translating Ruskin's *The Bible of Amiens*; he was interested in seeing the monuments Ruskin had described and analyzed in *Stones of Venice*. There was a second visit in October of that year, but no correspondence concerning it has survived. According to all reports, the May visit was about as cheerful as anything could be in Proust's life: his friends, Reynaldo Hahn and Reynaldo's cousin, Marie Nordlinger, were also in

Venice; the three young people explored Venice together. Proust's knowledge of English was at the time limited, and Marie helped with the proofs of his translation. Drastically changed, with Reynaldo and Marie expunged and the mother very much present, the May visit becomes a pivotal episode in *La fugitive*, which was published twenty-five years later, in 1925. Proust did not live to correct the proofs of that work; at the time of his death, in 1922, he was still revising the manuscript.

La fugitive is the sixth and next to last volume of *À la recherche du temps perdu*. Proust considered it the most beautiful text he had written. The fugitive referred to by the title is Albertine, one of the *jeunes filles en fleur*, enchanting adolescents, whom the Narrator, an adolescent himself, precocious and sickly, meets on the boardwalk of Balbec. He falls in love with her desperately and morbidly, but only after he has become jealous and suspicious of her. In *La prisonnière*, the volume that precedes

La fugitive, Albertine quite improbably comes to live with the Narrator – as his mistress – in the room adjoining his in the apartment of Narrator's parents. How a young woman of respectable bourgeoisie, even if she was a poor orphan like Albertine, could possibly be a part of such an arrangement in French society at the beginning of the twentieth century is a mystery; we make a leap of faith to accept it. The Narrator subjects her to constant surveillance: the chauffeur he employs, her best friend, Andrée, another of the *jeunes filles en fleur*, and even the redoubtable family retainer, Françoise, are all asked to spy on her. Albertine becomes the Narrator's prisoner. His jealousy is as unbearable to her as it is to him; his suspicions that she may have lesbian affairs, and his clumsy efforts to uncover them, his threats – he likes to frighten her by saying they must break up, and then, when she has been browbeaten into submission, to stage a provisional reconciliation – finally exhaust her patience. At the end of *La prisonière*, after one more atrocious scene, the exhausted and satisfied Narrator sleeps late. When he finally awakens, he rings for Françoise, who informs him that "Mlle Albertine asked for her trunks...she left at nine." The prisoner has become a fugitive! This is a fatal blow, and also a *coup de théâtre*, because at the conclusion of the previous evening's scene, confident that once again he had Albertine under his control, the Narrator decided that he would leave, without saying goodbye, for Venice, since many years the city of his dreams. Indeed, when he summoned Françoise, it was with the intention of sending her out to buy a guide to Venice and get him the train schedules. *La fugitive* is the story of the aftermath: the Narrator learns that Albertine has been killed in a riding accident; he makes new futile efforts to ferret out the secrets of her past; he mourns her. And in Venice he makes the shattering discovery that he has forgotten her.

On what do I base my claim that the May 1900 visit to Venice as it appears in *La fugitive* has a pivotal significance in *À la recherche*?

To answer this question it is necessary to take into account the extraordinary, totemic importance of Venice in Proust's work. In *Du côté de chez Swann,* an illness prevents an Easter trip to Venice that the Narrator, then a small boy, has been promised. In his imagination, Venice becomes a pendant to the mythical Balbec and its "Persian" cathedral. But the Narrator's fervent wish to go to Balbec is fulfilled, because his parents think he will benefit from the climate. By contrast, bad health continues to frustrate his hopes of visiting Venice – or Florence or Padua and its Giotto frescoes of virtues and vices. Gradually, Venice becomes for the Narrator's mind the most exotic of cities, an aquatic Baghdad – a setting for the tales of another thousand and one nights of mysterious and furtive sexual adventures. He develops what can only be called a tic of thinking, whenever his jealousy of Albertine is momentarily appeased, and his infatuation with her recedes, jealousy being an indispensable prerequisite to love, that instead of being bored by the young woman's constant presence he could be in Venice alone, happy among the works of the masters he admires, and enjoying the favors of young working girls whose paths he would cross in the byways of the secret Venetian labyrinth. The frequency with which Venice is mentioned in *À la recherche* – twenty-three times in *La Prisonnière* alone – gives some measure of the Narrator's obsession.

The beginning of the Venetian section of *La fugitive* gives the reader an immediate signal that something is amiss during that finally accomplished visit:

> As for the third time when I remember having been conscious that I was approaching absolute indifference for

Albertine (and this last time to the extent of feeling that I had altogether reached it), it was one day in Venice, quite a while after Andrée's last visit. My mother had taken me there, and – as beauty can exist in the most humble things as well as in the most precious – I tasted there impressions I had so often felt in the past in Combray, but transposed in a manner entirely different and richer.

How is it, we are moved to ask, that this grown man needs to be "taken" by his mother to Venice? A man who has recently kept, for many months, a mistress in his parents' apartment, given her extraordinary toilettes and artistic objects, and seriously considered as additional gifts or bribes a Rolls Royce and a yacht, and, on the other side of the ledger, after the mistress's disappearance continued to have rather surprising sexual encounters, with very young girls, Andrée, and prostitutes, in the same parental apartment? The mother, by the way, had disappeared from view in *La prisonière,* except for an occasional plaintive letter, and her first reappearance in *La fugitive* is precisely this one. Can it really be that the first immediate association that occurs to the Narrator when at last he reaches mythical Venice is with Combray? (Combray is the invented little town in the Beauce region, part of the ducal domain of the Guermantes, where the Narrator's family has its roots, and where he has gone for holidays as a child. It stands, among other things, for values and codes of behavior that are historically and immutably French.). But that is indeed what has happened: upon seeing "the golden angel of the campanile of Saint Mark's," in the morning, when the chambermaid opens the shutters of his bedroom, the Narrator can only think how the architecture of Venice, and the life of the canals and the Piazza San Marco, echo the life of Combray. Of course, this is a bow in the direction of Ruskin, who thought that the architecture of gothic churches was an extension of domestic architecture, but the bow is too deep and too elaborate. Then, almost immediately, we encounter the mother, and the flood of the Narrator's tormented feelings about her. In a development of great beauty the Narrator speaks of the balcony of the hotel on the Grand Canal from the height of which she can keep an eye out for the gondola bringing him back for lunch after his morning outing. In turn, he can anticipate, as the gondola draws near, that he will see that the white scarf the mother hangs over the balcony's balustrade as a signal that he is present in her thoughts. It is also startling to find in Venice personages — the marquise de Villeparisis, the school friend of the Narrator's grandmother, M. de Norpois, the marquise's aged lover, and Madame Sazerat, a

Combray neighbor – who seemed to have vanished from the stage of *À la recherche*. They were not mentioned in *La prisonière*, and one might have imagined them dead. It is stranger still that the Narrator should eavesdrop in a restaurant on a long conversation between the marquise and M. de Norpois, and then between the old pair and an Italian diplomat who has come forward to greet the marquise. Is that not an obvious variation on the great scene in *Sodome et Gomorrhe,* in which the Narrator, concealed in the basement, spies on the first amorous encounter between Baron de Charlus and Jupien?

One may be tempted to suspect that these oddities are due to the posthumous publication of *La fugitive,* and Proust's not having come close to completing his revision of the manuscript (*La prisonière,* and the last volume of *À la recherche*, *Le temps retrouvé* were also published after Proust's death), or to find in them examples of Proust's compulsive use of certain devices – which include unexpected juxtapositions of landscapes, surprise meetings, and metamorphoses of characters – and to speculate that they would have disappeared from a corrected manuscript. I do not believe that; on the contrary, I think that, coming as they do in the midst of superb descriptions of Venice, these peculiarities are deliberate and essential clues intended to mark the Narrator's estrangement from the magnificence of the Venetian spectacle. That conclusion is consistent with the lessons the Narrator learns in Venice, and the progress he makes there toward the self-knowledge finally attained *Le temps retrouvé,* the last volume of *À la rercherche.*

The lesson I will mention first, because it concerns immediately Albertine, is that love can and does end completely, so that, if it turned out miraculously that Albertine was alive – which is what a garbled telegram the Narrator receives in his hotel seems to indicate – he would feel no joy. The reason for the extinction of love is tragically simple:

we change as time passes. The memory of persons we once loved is erased. The Narrator finds, in fact, that he is unable to remember Albertine. The work of time is inexorable. As the Narrator observes, "It is rare for a widower, or an inconsolable father, not to heal within the same length of time that it will take a patient stricken by cancer to die."

Second, he learns that there is one circumstance in which the memory of a person we loved in the past may survive: the coincidental association of the memory of that person with a work of art — works of art having an existence untouched by the vicissitudes of our memory. This lesson is learned in the course of the Narrator's visit with his mother to the Baptistery of Saint Mark's:

> Seeing that I would have to remain a long time before the mosaics that represent the baptism of Christ, my mother, who felt the icy chill that descended on us

in the Baptistery, would throw a shawl over my shoulders. When I was with Albertine in Balbec, I thought that she revealed one of those incoherent illusions that fill the minds of people who do not think clearly when she spoke to me of the pleasure – in my opinion based on nothing – that she would find in seeing a certain painting with me. Today, I am at least sure that such a pleasure exists, if not in seeing, then at least in having seen, a beautiful object with a particular person... [I]t is not indifferent to me, when I remember the baptistery, that in the cool half shade, there was at my side a woman draped in her mourning, with the respectful and enthusiastic fervor of the old woman one sees in Venice in the Saint Ursula of Carpaccio, and that this woman, with red cheeks and sad eyes, in her black veils, whom nothing can ever remove for me from that softly lit sanctuary of Saint Mark's, where I am sure of finding her because she has her place there reserved and unchanging like a mosaic, should be my mother.

Indeed, only once after the Narrator's discovery of the hard law of oblivion his love for Albertine comes close to reviving: that is when at the Accademia, in Carpaccio's painting of the Patriarch of Grado exorcising a demon, he notices, thrown over the shoulders of a Venetian nobleman, a coat that the great designer and couturier Fortuny had copied, and that he, the Narrator, had bought for Albertine. She wore it on their last evening together, driving out to Versailles. "I had recognized it all," the Narrator tells us, and the forgotten coat having given back to me, so that I could look at it, the eyes and the heart of him who was going to leave for Versailles that evening with Albertine, I was overcome for a short instant by a confused and soon dissipated feeling of desire and melancholy."

The third lesson has as its subject the complete insignificance of places – in the event, Venice – when they are emptied of the emotional content that only we can pour into them. That lesson is learned while the Narrator, having quarreled with his mother and told her that he will not return to Paris with her, sits on the terrace of his hotel, a drink on the table before him. A boat has stopped on the Canal in front of the hotel bearing a musician who sings *Sole mio*. The Narrator - a lover of the music of Vinteuil (an invented composer largely modeled on Franck and Wagner) is mesmerized by the vulgar song, and seems unable to stir, although he realizes that his mother must be reaching the railroad station, and that, unless he rushes there at once, he will be left in Venice, "alone with the knowledge of having caused her pain and without her presence to console me." While this paralysis of the will continues, he notes that

> things became estranged from me, I no longer had enough calm to step outside of my palpitating heart and introduce into them any stability. The city I had before me had stopped being Venice. Its personality, its name, seemed to me mendacious fictions that I no longer had the courage to inculcate in stones. The palaces seemed to me reduced to their simple parts and quantities of marble similar to any other, and water a combination of hydrogen and oxygen

and nitrogen, eternal, blind, anterior and exterior to Venice, ignorant of the Doges and Turner. And yet this insignificant place was strange like a place where you arrive and which does not yet know you, like a place that you have left and that has already forgotten you. I could no longer say anything to it about myself, leave anything of myself to settle on it, it contracted upon me, I was nothing more but a beating heart and an attention that followed anxiously the development of *Sole mio.* It was no use trying desperately to attach my thought to the beautiful curve characteristic of the Rialto, it appeared to me only with the evident mediocrity of a bridge not only inferior to the idea I had of it but also estranged from it, like an actor of whom we know that, in spite of his blond wig and black costume, in his essence he is not Hamlet. So the palaces, the Canal, the Rialto, stripped of the idea that made their individuality, all dissolved into their vulgar, material elements.

What role has been assigned to Venice in this episode? I believe that it is to demonstrate conclusively its own intrinsic insignificance, except as a receptacle for what the Narrator – and, by extension, the reader – may bring to the experience of being there. The visit to Venice marks the definitive turning inward of Proust's novel. From that point on, the stage is no longer the exterior world of names and places that so enchanted the Narrator at the outset of his life journey; it is the interior world of his consciousness. It is an essential, and meticulously planned role, as important in *À la recherche* as the role played by Venice in *The Wings*. Venice will return in all its importance during the great epiphany scene in *Le temps retrouvé*, the concluding volume of *À la recherche*, when the memory of the uneven stone floor of the Baptistery of St. Marks reveals to the Narrator the reality of his literary vocation and the means through which to fulfill it.

Paradoxically, most of the action of Thomas Mann's famous novella, *Death in Venice*, which may be the best-known treatment of Venice in fiction, takes place on the Lido, and not in the city itself; indeed, the protagonist, Gustav von Aschenbach, does not die in Venice. He dies on the beach in Lido. Death in Venice is not Aschenbach's death; it is the deadly plague that invests the city.

Aschenbach is a celebrated German writer in his early fifties, living in Munich, rather like Mann but considerably older, since in 1911, when he began to write *Death in Venice,* Mann was only thirty-five. Through unremitting hard work and self-discipline, Aschenbach has turned himself into the exemplary established author, the polished traditionalist, conservative, formal, even formulaic; and as the story about Louis XIV goes, the aging man banished all vulgar words from his vocabulary.

Mann's ironic tone of voice underscores this further point of resemblance. At the moment, however, Aschenbach has difficulty making progress on a work he is writing. He thinks that

> No unusual difficulty was involved: instead he was being paralyzed by a scruple born of aversion, taking the form of a fastidious dissatisfaction that could no longer be dispelled by any means... Were his enslaved emotions now taking their toll by abandoning him, by refusing to further his art and lend it wings...

While the nation honored his status as a
master, he himself had no joy in it, as if
his work lacked those tokens of fiery,
playful spontaneity which were a result
of joy...and so a parenthesis was necessary, a bit of impromptu existence, some
loafing, an exotic atmosphere, if the
summer was to be bearable and pro-
ductive. Travel then — he was satisfied
with the idea. Not very far... One night
in a sleeper and a siesta of three or four
weeks at some well-known holiday
resort in the charming south of Europe.

At first he travels to an island off the coast of Istria.
He finds he dislikes it. Feeling "an inner compulsion
to move," he studies ship connections, and

all at once, surprising and at the same
time self-evident, he saw his goal before

him. If you wanted to reach some place overnight that was incomparable, different as a fairy tale where would you go?

The answer is Venice, or as it turns out the Lido, and the Hôtel des Bains, where Aschenbach finds the bewitching Tadzio, a fourteen year old, incredibly beautiful, pale, blond and delicate Polish boy of noble family, staying there with his mother, older sisters and governess. Aschenbach falls in love heels over head. He cannot take his eyes off Tadzio at the beach, follows him when the boy and his family go for excursions in Venice, and permits himself never before imagined indiscretions. As Aschenbach's passion grows, the weather in Venice turns hot and sultry; the sirocco blows; the sky is leaden. Aschenbach knows that he should leave. He hasn't found at the Lido the health and new energy he had hoped for; indeed, he feels increasingly oppressed. But he lacks the resolve to leave while Tadzio is still there. Weeks pass. There is sickening smell of disinfectant in Venice. Aschenbach's suspicions are aroused. Remarks of the hotel barber and more or less veiled reports in the German press add to them. A conversation with an English clerk in a travel agency, "a man with that sedate honesty of character which strikes one as so different and peculiar when encountered in the scoundrelly supersubtle south of Europe," removes any ambiguity. There is an epidemic of Indian cholera in the city that the authorities, afraid that tourists will flee, have been trying to conceal. Meanwhile, the clerk says,

> the prevailing insecurity...that the stalking death had brought forth in the city, resulted in a certain demoralization of the lower classes, an incitement to criminal and antisocial impulses which took the form of intemperance, shame-less behavior, and a growing crime rate...

professional vice took on conspicuous, excessive proportions hitherto unknown here, and at home only in the south of the country and in the Orient.

"You would do well," he advises Aschenbach, "to leave today rather than tomorrow."

Aschenbach considers this advice, as well as the need to take

an action that would be cleansing and decent. After dinner...he could go up to the [Polish] lady...and deliver the speech he was now sketching out word for word: "Please permit a stranger, Madame, to give you a piece of advice, a warning ... Leave, and right away, with Tadzio and your daughters: Venice is plague-stricken." But at the same time he felt that he was infinitely far from seriously wishing to take such a step. It would recall him to his senses, it would restore him to himself; but a man who is beside himself dreads nothing worse than to become himself again ... the idea of returning home, acting, sensibly, sobering up, and resuming his labours ... was so repellent to him that his face contorted into an expression of physical nausea. "They want people to keep quiet!" he whispered violently. And added: "I *will* keep quiet!" The consciousness that he was an accessory to the secret, and equally guilty, intoxicated him ... The image of the afflicted and neglected city... kindled his hopes that bypassed reason and were tremendously sweet ... What were art and virtue to him any longer in contrast with the advantages of chaos? He kept silent and he stayed on.

At this point, Aschenbach's moral collapse has become complete, and it is reflected in his bearing. He allows the hotel barber to apply makeup to his face, pluck his eyebrows, and dye his hair; he makes eye contact with Tadzio as he follows him and his family through Venice; he has "unsavory hopes." One night, he dreams of a Panic orgy of extraordinary dimensions and violence. Hirsute and bestial followers celebrate Dionysius; his obscene wooden symbol is unveiled and uplifted. Aschenbach takes part. He is

> now with them, one of them, a slave of the foreign god. Yes, they were his own self as they flung themselves upon the animals, tearing and killing, swallowing scraps of flesh that were still smoking, while an unbridled coupling began on the trampled mossy ground, as an offering to the god. And his soul tasted the lewdness and frenzy of extinction.

A few days later, feeling indisposed, "suffering from certain attacks of dizziness which were only partially physical," Aschenbach comes down to the hotel lobby later than usual and learns that the Polish noble family is leaving after lunch. Their trunks are in the hall. That leaves him little time. He hurries to the beach, sits down in his reclining chair, and, as usual, watches Tadzio and his friends. There is a struggle, not entirely playful, between Tadzio and an older boy, which alarms Aschenbach; the older boy pins Tadzio down on the sand. When he lets him go, the beautiful child walks away toward a sandbar. From there, he looks back toward the shore, and it

> seemed [to Aschenbach] ... as if the pale charming psychagogue out there were smiling to him, beckoning to him; as if he were raising his hand from his hip and pointing outward, floating before him into a realm of promise and

immensity. And as he had done so often, [Aschenbach] set out to follow him.

Mann has thus signaled the novella's abrupt ending. A psychagogue is one who, like Hermes, leads the souls of the newly dead to the world beyond:

> Minutes went by before people hastened to the aid of the man who had slumped sideways in his chair. He was carried to his room. And before that day was over a respectfully shocked world received news of his death.

The correlation between *Death in Venice* and Mann's life is, of course, striking. Mann was a life-long bisexual, who fathered six children notwithstanding a marked, abiding and carefully concealed preference for boys and young men. Neither his taste nor his specific attachments became widely known until 1975, twenty years after his death, when some five thousand pages of journals that he did not destroy became available. Mann visited Venice several times. The trip to Venice, or rather Lido, which resembles Aschenbach's, took place in 1911. Mann and his wife Katia began their summer vacation on Brioni – the island to which Aschenbach also travels first – but the weather and the rocky beaches disappointed them, just like his protagonist. They too left for the Lido, arriving in Venice by boat, like Aschenbach, and like him they stayed at the Hôtel des Bains. Moreover, among the guests of the hotel, there was a Polish family with a beautiful, spoiled and at the time sickly eleven-year-old boy – not Tadzio but Władzio, or, to give his full name, Władysław Moes. Władzio recognized himself in Mann's novella, when it appeared in 1923 in Polish translation, and recalled the "old man" who never took his eyes off him, wherever he went.

There was no plague in Venice in 1911. However, there was an epidemic of cholera, in Palermo.

I am now obliged to turn to the question I have set for myself: what use did Mann make of Venice in this very complex story, beyond describing it with matchless grace? One example of the marvels of his writing may suffice. Here is Aschenbach, on the deck of the steamer he boarded after the failed vacation on the island off Istria, arriving at the Riva degli Schiavoni:

> he saw it again, that most amazing landing place, that dazzling composition of fantastic architecture which the Republic presented to the reverent gaze of approaching seafarers; the weightless splendor of the Palace, the Bridge of Sighs, the columns with lion and saint on the bank, the ostentatiously projecting side of the fairy-tale temple, the view

through the gateway and the giant clock, and as he gazed, he reflected that to arrive by land, at the Venice railroad station, was like entering a palace through a back door, and that the only proper way to approach that most improbable of cities was that by which he had now come, by ship, across the open sea.

The answer is that Mann uses Venice as a brilliant metaphor, a city turned into a fever chart tracing Aschenbach's moral disintegration and the victory of Dionysius, the rough, foreign God, over the stern writer. The dichotomy between the Apollonian and the Dionysian principles is near the surface of most of Mann's fiction, as is the struggle of the artist drawn by the Dionysian, but duty bound to resist, and to cleave to the Apollonian principle. Nothing in the struggle is clear. How far should the artist yield to the temptation of freedom and, indeed, disorder? At what point, if he holds himself in check, is he menaced by the loss of spontaneity and joy? Aschenbach's catastrophe comes upon him because he allows passion to carry him too far; he takes the bait set by the foreign god.

Here is how Mann's Venice illustrates Aschenbach's accelerating decline. As soon as Aschenbach falls under Tadzio's spell, the weather turns:

> The wind blew from the land. Beneath a livid, overcast sky the sea lay in a dull calm, as if shrunken, with an uninterestingly close horizon, and it had receded so far from the beach that several tiers of long sandbars were left exposed. When Aschenbach opened his window, he thought he could smell the putrid odor of the lagoon.

When Tadzio stands close to Aschenbach in the hotel lift, he notices that the boys teeth

> were not that fine: a little jagged and pale, lacking the glow of health. "He is very delicate, he is sickly," thought Aschenbach, "He probably won't live to a ripe old age." And he avoided accounting to himself for the feeling of satisfaction or consolation that accompanied that thought.

That afternoon, he takes the "vaporetto across the ill-smelling lagoon to Venice." He does not yet suspect the presence of the epidemic, and, after tea in the Piazza San Marco, he takes a walk through the city:

> The narrow streets were unpleasantly sultry; the air was so thick that the

odors emanating from homes, stores and cookshops – olive oil, clouds of perfume, and many others – hung like wisps of smoke without being dispersed. Cigarette smoke remained in place and drifted away only slowly. The jostling in narrow passages annoyed him instead of amusing him as he strolled. The longer he walked, the more tormented he became by the horrible state of health that the sea air can cause in conjunction with the sirocco, a state of excitement and prostration at the same time. His eyes no longer performed their duty, he felt a tightness in his chest, he was feverish, the blood pounded in his head. He fled from the crowded shopping streets across bridges into the haunts of the poor. There he was importuned by beggars, and the foul effluvia of the canals made breathing a torture. On a quiet square, one of those spots deep within Venice that give the impression of being forgotten under an evil spell, he rested by the rim of a fountain, dried his forehead, and realized that he had to go away.

In this state, he arrives at the Piazza San Marco, from where,

At the nearest gondola landing he boarded a boat and made his way through the gloomy labyrinth of the canals, under ornamental marble balconies flanked by statues of lions, around greasy corners of walls, past mournful palace facades that reflected large commercial signs in the garbage-strewn, rocking water...whenever the bizarre ride through Venice began to exert its magic, the money grabbing business mentality of the fallen queen did its part to bring him back to reality in a painful way.

Later, his plan to leave Venice abandoned, Aschenbach realizes that even the "slightly foul odor of sea and swamp" is dear to him; he breathes it in deeply. And he goes on watching Tadzio:

> Soon the observer knew every line and pose of that body which was so elegant, which offered itself so freely; with joy he greeted anew each already familiar detail of his beauty; there was no end to his admiration, his delicate sensual pleasure.

When he begins to suspect the epidemic, Aschenbach

> felt a hidden satisfaction with the events in the dirty alleys of Venice that were

being covered up by the authorities —
this criminal secret of the city which
coincided with his own dark secret...

On a Sunday, he follows the Polish family to mass
at St. Mark's. Afterward the family takes a gondola,
apparently for a tour of the canals; Aschenbach
hires one himself and tells the gondolier to follow
discreetly — the man assures him "with a pander's
villainous alacrity," that he will. They glide past
picture postcard views, and Aschenbach tells himself

That was Venice, the obsequious and
un-trustworthy beauty — this city, half
fairy tale, half tourist, in whose reeking
atmosphere art had once extravagantly
luxuriated...

The title of the novella, the plague in the city, and
Aschenbach's death on the Lido beach, in a last

effort to follow his charming psychagogue, round out Mann's inspired metaphor.

During 1997, I wrote my own "Venetian" novel, *Mistler's Exit*, first published in 1998. Its action begins in New York, when the protagonist, Thomas Mistler, an advertising mogul of exceptional talent and considerable glamour, learns from his doctor that he has cancer of the liver. If he refuses the operation, chemotherapy, radiation and other beneficent torments, which is Mistler's instant and irreversible decision, he has some six months to live. Mistler is in his early sixties, a saturnine, domineering and physically powerful man married to a woman he doesn't much love or respect. He does love deeply, perhaps reverently, his only son, but their relations are tense, strained by feelings of guilt. Faced with the news, Mistler preposterously, unmistakably ... began to rejoice. The horizon would no longer recede. The space and time left to him were defined; he had been set free.

It occurs to him that, while he still feels well, before he enters what his doctor calls the "war zone," he is entitled to a special treat, something to savor in the time of grace that remains to him. He decides on ten days of serene emptiness in Venice,

the one place on earth where nothing irritated him. Neither research nor planning was required. He knew where to stay and which room to ask for and how to avoid the tourists who feed pigeons at San Marco or follow, like an ugly ship in the wake of the pilot's tug, some garrulous, polyglot person with a funny-colored open umbrella.

Not surprisingly, he decides to go alone, before he has told his wife or son; a long weekend or a week with them devoted to discussions of the cancer isn't his idea of a treat.

So then the action shifts to Venice. Mistler wanders about the city, has a sort of four-night stand with a young woman who, uninvited, debarks in his hotel-room, after a forty-year hiatus meets unexpectedly the first girl he had ever loved, struggles with memories of his parents, and wife, and a former partner who was also a former best friend, and perhaps finds a way to come to terms with his son. In the afternoon of his last day, after saying goodbye to his first love, on his way back to his hotel from the Giudecca where the long-lost love lives, he decides he will not climb once more the steps of the Accademia Bridge or thread his way through the crowd of the Senegalese chattering among their wares in Campo San Stefano. He will instead walk along the

Zattere toward the Dogana, round the point, and stop at the Salute, if it is open, to take a farewell look at the Titian ceilings. Afterward, he will board the *traghetto*; he hopes it will be in service.

But before he reaches the Dogana, the Buccintore rowing club arrests his attention. Mistler is an accomplished oarsman, and falls into conversation with a small, dark-skinned old man sitting on the quay, outside the club, while he repairs an oarlock. The single sculls and the great racing eights are on view behind him. The man invites Mistler to stop by the next day; there will be a race and, if a member of one of the crews is absent, perhaps Mistler will be willing to replace him. Tomorrow is too late, Mistler replies, but having looked carefully at the passage between at San Giorgio and the Giudecca, he wonders whether this invitation is not a sign. He asks whether he might be able to buy a single scull. There isn't one for sale, he is told, but the old man offers to sell him a wherry

— "squat and shiny black like a long coffin."
Mistler recognizes the virtues of this vessel:

> One might go to sea in it when the
> days grow short, in the early evening,
> an hour or so before sunset, just as the
> wind fell. The end of the Giudecca to
> starboard, pass out of sight and out of
> mind. Ahead lies the Lido. At its end,
> San Pietro in Volta ... Between them
> the narrow passage of Malamocco ...
> The last rays of the sun in your eyes,
> the prow points at the place from
> which the moon will rise. The watery
> space is vast.

The sale is closed, and Mistler's obol changes
hands. The reader has witnessed the staging of
what may or may not be in some months, or sooner,
or later, Mistler's exit.

Why did I set my story in Venice? I had been thinking for some time about what a protagonist like Mistler might do if suddenly and unexpectedly he learned that he would be dead within a very short period of time, and for the moment felt well, so that neither the operating table nor an exit of his own devising, seemed immediately necessary. That was the predicament I wanted to deal with. Sometimes, I would say to myself that the protagonist would simply do the things he normally did: keep his New York residence, go to the office, and drive to the country for the weekend. There would be one important change: he might wish to spend much more time with his wife, if it turned out that the protaginist and his wife loved each other. Perhaps they would have lunch together every day.

The thought did come to me though – in the brief periods of bitterness that such reflections induce – that such a man might want to have a few days off during which he might examine his conscience without having at hand a witness he knows and loves, a witness who knows him so well that very little that passes through his mind can remain hidden. Inevitably, I thought of Venice as a place for such a retreat, because nothing about Venice irritates me, and I know Venice well enough to be able to treat it casually, like an old friend with whom one doesn't need to make conversation through compulsive attendance at museums, churches and other indispensable monuments. I was certain that that my protagonist would feel the same. The other themes of the book — especially relations between a father and his children, the uses of power, and the devastation by power of those who use it — are obsessions that surface in one form or another in all my novels. And so I decided that my protagonist would go to Venice and suffer his agony there.

Of course, I was aware of the novels of my great predecessors who had used Venice as a setting, especially Thomas Mann, since I would be in a sense writing against him. In fact, I had gone as far as to borrow Mann's initials and give them to my man. My Thomas Mistler too might perhaps have been a writer, but he gave up after a discouraging start. In his own way, however, he had worked as hard as Aschenbach at his kind of illusionism, and adhered to a form of Apollonian discipline. Aschenbach came to Venice hoping to be reinvigorated and found death on the Lido; Mistler would come face to face with his death in New York, and find in Venice a clearer view of life. I did not feel that I had to measure my evocation of Venice against the work of great masters, and I knew I would enjoy trying to make the "city of exhibition" rise on my own pages.

The use I have made of Venice is not unlike Proust's: Venice, which Mistler loves, is there before his eyes. He sees it clearly and is moved and amused by it. But he is at a pass when everything external to his unfinished business – principally his relationship with his son – is only an ironic accompaniment to his thoughts. But no ordinary place, in fact no place that I can think of other than Venice, would have provided an accompaniment that is as beautiful, or creates a more dramatic contrast between interior and exterior realities.

As I reread *The Aspern Papers, The Wings of the Dove, La fugitive* and *Death in Venice,* I was struck by how very little that is intrinsically Venetian has changed over the last one hundred and fifty years, and yet the city is no more a museum or a stage set than it was when Milly Theale came to "live, if she could only manage it," in the Palazzo Leporelli. Except in one respect: the gondola, which with its gondolier braying into a microphone *Sole Mio* or *Santa Lucia,* two marvelously un-Venetian airs, for the benefit of comatose tourists, has to my mind become a pest equaled only by the pigeons of San Marco. Never mind if Proust called the pigeons

the lilies of Venice. Or that in *Italian Hours,* you
will find Henry James counseling that

> [t]he gondolier is your very good friend
> … He is part of your daily life, your
> double, your shadow, your complement.

Milly has two gondolas and two gondoliers constantly at her beck and call. When Merton
Densher is denied access to the palace, and therefore the use of the gondolas, and is reduced to
getting about on foot, he feels bitter about the
degradation, rather like a down-at-the-heels, aging
New York beau when no one thinks to send a
radio car to take him to a party. The Narrator in
La fugitive goes everywhere by gondola. He hints
darkly at expeditions on foot in search of working
girls in abandoned *campi* and *rii,* but I don't believe
a word of it. I think that, just as for Aschenbach,
some gondolier was the alacritous pander for the

Narrator. When I first came to Venice, half a century ago, on an early summer morning, I took a gondola from the railroad station to San Marco, in the proximity of which was the fleabag where I was to stay. That gondola trip is the one extravagance I have never regretted. It doesn't even occur to Mistler to hire a gondola; instead, rather like me in this, when he isn't on foot he takes the *vaporetto*, nowadays my favorite mode of transportation, and those are times when, also like me, he amuses himself by not paying the boatman his obol.